BETH

by

Elizabeth Manwaring

BETH
By

Elizabeth Manwaring

Copyright Information

All rights reserved. No part of this publication may be reproduced or stored in a retrieval system, rebound or transmitted in any form or for any purpose without the prior written permission of the author and publisher. This book is sold subject to the condition that it shall not be lent, resold, hired out or otherwise circulated without the publisher's prior consent in any form or binding other than that in which it is published.

Re-published by:

Harvey Harman

2014

h.harman@sky.com

Acknowledgements

I wish to thank Patrick Cox-Smith for his meticulous reading of the final script and his help with his experience of farming.

I also wish to thank my husband, Len and my friend Juliette Vane for their help and encouragement.

I acknowledge the help 1 found in 'The Farmer' by Helen Holt.
Education Supply Association Ltd 1952

Dedication

I dedicate this book in memory of my mother

INTRODUCTION

Elizabeth Mayfield, known as Beth, remembers when England declared war on Germany. Her story is based on a child's experience as an evacuee, living on a farm in Devonshire during the war between the years 1939-1945. Beth's story begins in September 1939 when she was evacuated with her mother, sister and brother along with so many other children from London. Her father stayed behind to work at Croydon aerodrome 'to help with the war effort.'

This book tells of her life at that time, of leaving her home in Croydon, South London with all the noise and destruction caused by the war and the extreme contrast of living on a farm in the peaceful countryside of North Devon. It describes the farm and the people who lived there, their daily life and seasonal work. The farm was called Lydacott. The farmhouse and its buildings stood on a hill where the fields sloped gently down to a stream and the village of Fremington. Lydacott was a mixed farm of animals and crops that belonged to Walter Bale and his wife Rose. They had no children of their own so were happy to take in Beth, her sister, brother and mother during the war.

The story continues with the evacuees adapting to their completely new way of life and the years that followed in which the children grew and matured in their formative years away from the horrors of war.

The realization when the war was over that they had to return to their home in Croydon and to their father was unbearable for them. The close relationships and hopes they had made are interwoven with their love of the farm. It was to be a devastating experience for them all when they did return and the events that took place were to change their lives forever.

Contents

Chapter		
1	Unknown Destination	7
2	Making Friends	12
3	School Days	17
4	Christmas Joy	22
5	The Promise of Spring	29
6	The Surprise	35
7	Haymaking	41
8	Father's Visit	46
9	Barnstable Market	53
10	Harvesting the Corn	56
11	Harvest Festival	61
12	Farewell Lydacott	64
13	Returning Home	68
14	Nitty Nora	75
15	Father's Fury	83
16	The Letter	90
17	The Girl Friend	98
18	Mixed Emotions	105
19	Andrew's secret	111
20	Friends	116
21	Future Hopes	122
22	The Surprise Visitor	130
23	The Visit	137
24	Troubled Times	144
25	A New Encounter	148
26	A New Beginning	154

Chapter 1
Unknown Destination

Amid the menacing sound of air-raid sirens and people rushing on to the platform at West Croydon railway station, Beth, her mother, sister and brother boarded the train to Devonshire. The children were excited as it was like going on a holiday. Her mother, they were told later, enlisted as a volunteer worker to stay with them through that troubled time. It was a long journey as they watched the scene change from being a built up area of streets and houses to the open greenery of the countryside. They saw fields and trees and animals that they had only seen before in their picture books. It was an exciting and happy journey for them all.

At last the train puffed and hissed to a stop. It was cold but the platform was bathed in sunshine as they jumped out of the train at Barnstable station that September afternoon. Taking her young son by the hand their mother said they were to wait at the side of the platform. At that moment a lady and gentleman came up to them and with a broad Devonshire accent the man asked them if they would like to come and stay with them on their farm in Fremington. The couple had seen the evacuee labels on the children and thought they would like somewhere to stay. The anxious look left their mothers eyes as she looked at the friendly faces and she happily accepted their kind offer. The children were excited to think they were going to live on a farm and were full of questions.

Later they were told that Mr and Mrs Bale were on the same train as themselves and were returning home from London after visiting Mrs Bale's sister who was very ill. Having no children of their own, they were considering taking in an evacuee. By chance they saw a slightly built, attractive lady with three pale looking children. They thought it could be beneficial for them to live on a farm and the lady would be a great help to Mrs Bale so they asked the family if they would like to go and stay with them for the duration of the war.

It was only a short journey by car from the station to Lydacott Farm. The sun was still shining when they stopped outside a five-bar gate. The gate opened onto an unmade path leading to the farm house. As they walked toward the house and farmyard they were suddenly startled by the noisy quacking and hissing of geese and ducks. The ducks had come through a large hole in an old stone wall beside the path. The children were frightened at first and Mr Bale explained that they must be very wary of them, as geese were quite vicious. They didn't like intruders and that is why he kept them. When reaching the house they heard dogs barking furiously and many chickens squawked and fluttered out of the way as they entered the courtyard. The children thought they had been transported into another world.

There were also lots of cats and kittens, some eating and drinking around the open door leading into the house. The family were told later that most of them were wild. 'Uncle Walter' and 'Aunt Rose' as the family came to know Mr and Mrs Bale, welcomed them in. The family were amazed as they entered a large room that had a stone floor, which had an open 'inglenook' fire-place with a seat on either side. 'Our foreman Derek has made a nice fire up for us so I will put the kettle on for tea,' said Aunt Rose. She put the kettle on a hook over the fire and with a pair of bellows puffed the fire until the flames started going again. Beth thought how different this was going to be from their home and their little fireplace in Croydon. Although they were all tired after their long journey Ronald, Beth and her elder sister Anne felt they could not wait to explore their new surroundings but that had to wait until morning.

After the children had eaten. Aunt Rose showed them their rooms upstairs. The girls were to share a bedroom. They were given a double bed that had a brass bedstead. The bed had a pretty eiderdown on it and there was a wardrobe and dressing table. The room looked very neat and cosy. Through the window one could see the farm was situated high up on a hillside overlooking the down land and the village below. The girls came to love sitting on the window-seat and looking out at the wonderful view. Aunt Rose explained that there was no electricity or running water at the house and that the toilet was outside on the other side of the courtyard but as it was night time they were to use a chamber pot. Ronald who was only seven years old thought it was very funny, as they had not used one before. In the corner was a marble-topped washstand with a white china bowl and jug and above this was an embroidered text that read 'Home Sweet Home'.

An odd saying Beth thought, after their life at home in Croydon that had been far from sweet.

The sisters went to bed that night thinking how lucky they were that this was going to be their home. They felt safe now that they were not in London and wondered if they would need their gas masks there. Beth thought of her school and what the head master had said to everyone on their last day of assembly. Among other things he said. 'You are to be evacuated to the country because of the danger of enemy action and as evacuees you should follow certain rules of the countryside. You will see many different animals and should make sure that
you never leave any gates open. 'The girls noticed how quiet it was away from the noise and destruction of the war and snuggled down in their bed and feeling very tired, they fell blissfully asleep.

The next morning the girls woke up to a sound that made Beth laugh. Anne said it was a cockerel crowing. It was a sound they were to get used to hearing every morning. The girls soon washed and dressed and hurried downstairs. The smell of cooking made them feel hungry as they entered the large room. The warmth of the great open log fire surrounded them. Mother and Aunt Rose were preparing breakfast and called 'good morning' from the kitchen. A small table was set for breakfast and as they sat down they noticed on the walls were pictures of people that had worked on the land and farm in the past. There were oak beams everywhere and Beth wondered if anything had changed since the farm had been built, which must have been many years ago.

On the other side of the room stood a very long table with a bench seat on each side. A dresser stood nearby with open shelves that were full of china, with rows of cups hanging on brass hooks. They came to know this was for everyday use. On the floor were some colourful rugs similar to those which grandma had made from odd strips of material in Croydon. There were three doors and they were soon to discover that one led to the hall, another to the dairy and kitchen and one led to the scullery that had a door leading outside to the courtyard. The scullery had a tiled floor and a large sink where they were told all the household washing could be done.

The girls were too excited to sit at the table and went to find their mother who was happily busying herself in the kitchen. It was very large and not a bit like the one they had at home that was small. 'Did you sleep well? Your brother has already had his breakfast and has gone over to the barn,' said aunty, who was putting their breakfast onto a plate from a very big stove that seem to heat the room. 'Yes, thank you, it was a very comfortable bed and we love the room,' said Anne excitedly. The girls could not help noticing her larder was big enough to walk into with shelves all round it. 'The hooks on the ceiling are for hanging ham,' explained Aunt Rose. It was filled with food, more than the sisters had ever seen before. There was also a deep sink with a draining board each side.

'Come along and have your breakfast, there will be plenty of time to see everything,' said aunty. 'Uncle Walter will be coming in for his meal anytime now. He is always up first in the mornings,' she continued with a smile. 'He was up at five o'clock while you were still sleeping. 'The girls could not believe their eyes when they saw their huge cooked breakfast. It was a luxury that they were to get used to. When they thanked aunty, she said she always made a hearty breakfast as it was needed when you lived and worked on a farm. The girls were finishing their breakfast when uncle Walter came in with his two favourite dogs, Sheep and Honey. The girls heard the sound of his hob nailed boots on the stone floor that became a familiar sound to them and thought he had a kind weathered face and a beaming smile.

'Good morning. Well the sun is shining for you but there is a cool breeze so you will need your coats and hats. I expect you will be off soon to explore so be careful won't you. I have asked Derek's boys to look out for you. A farm is not really a place for children who have not been brought up on one,' he said with a smile, taking off his coat. He went over and sat down in his special seat in front of the fire, a real old fashioned chair. He then lit his pipe and gazed thoughtfully into the flames as if to think on the chores he had to do that day.

A typical evacuation train

Chapter 2
Making Friends

The girls soon found their coats and ran outside to join their brother. 'You must be the new evacuees,' a boy's voice called over from the other side of the courtyard. 'I'm Andrew Clayton and this is my sheepdog Pip. I live in the cottage over there,' he said, pointing to the other side of the farm. 'My father is Mr Bale's foreman and he helps run the farm.'

'I'm Beth and this is my sister Anne and brother Ronald.' Beth who was ten at that time was surprised at meeting anyone about her own age.

'You must make friends with Pip. 'Andrew continued. 'He can drive a flock of sheep into a field by himself and my dad could not do his work without him.' Secretly, Beth wondered what she could say to a dog that was barking at her.

'Would you like to look around the farm, 'Andrew asked.

'Oh yes please,' said Ronald. 'Do you have any pigs here? I'd like to see them.'

'We've lots,' said Andrew and led the way to the pigsty that was quite near the courtyard. As they all peered over the sty there were some pigs snorting about for food.

'Oh they are funny Look at their tails,' Beth cried, as one came up to them sniffing for something to eat.

'They are nice and clean,' exclaimed Anne, 'I thought pigs were always dirty and covered in mud. 'Anne didn't like anything dirty.

Andrew laughed. 'Pigs are clean animals really'

Anne and Beth looked at each other in disbelief as they watched him pick up a pail of food and put it in a dirty trough. Ronald gave a shrill of delight when he heard the pigs' squeals and grunts as they scoffed down their meal. 'Why are some pigs in individual stalls,' asked Anne. Andrew explained that it ensured that each sow got her own amount of food, without the stronger ones taking it from her.

'Let me show you one of the barns,' said Andrew, who seemed to be enjoying his new company. As they went over to the barn Andrew said that he lived with his elder brother Patrick, his mother Valerie and father Derek. All helped on the farm except his mother who helped occasionally as there was always plenty to do at their cottage and smallholding. The children entered the barn. It had a nice smell about it. There were sheep pens and some bales of hay and they disturbed some chickens that were nesting there. 'Some chickens prefer to lay their eggs on hay, especially in the dark corners of the barn instead of their nest-boxes,' said Andrew. He went on to explain that the hay was from the spring harvest, stored in the barn for feeding the cattle in winter when there was no grass in the fields. Beth could see there was a lot to farming. She was interested and eager to learn all she could.

Ronald wanted to jump on the bales but did not as he was trying to be on his best behaviour, which his sisters knew would not last and that he would be back to climb them when no one was looking. They went out into the sunshine again and Andrew took them down to an orchard. He said the apples were not ready for picking yet but when they were they might like to help with the harvest if they wanted to. Beth and Anne gazed at him and Anne remarked, 'You know so much about the farm Andrew, I'm afraid we have a lot to learn.'

'It is because I was born here, I suppose,' he explained, feeling a little embarrassed.

'I think we ought to go back now, it must be nearly dinner time,' said Beth, seeing her brother wanting to go scrumping. They thanked Andrew and as they walked back to the house, Beth looked back at Andrew with Pip standing by his side and felt happy they had made a new friend.

After dinner Ronald and Beth went over to explore the old open barn, opposite the house. Inside were all kinds of machinery that they had not seen before. There were two big wagons. Beth joined her brother as he jumped up on to one of them. Above them were some old beams from which Uncle Walter later put some rope and made them a swing. There was also an old tractor. 'Perhaps we will be able to ride on it,' Ronald said hopefully.

Note: Mealtimes were breakfast, dinner at midday, early evening tea and supper.

Anne came over from the house and joined them in the barn. 'Shall we go along the lane to the top field, I overheard uncle Walter say that the horses were kept
there and that you could see for miles,' said Anne with excitement. As they walked down the lane, Beth told Anne about all the exciting things to be found in the barn. Not to be left out Ronald told her about the tractor.

'1 wonder if we can help on the farm,' she said, longing to do something different from the life they had at Croydon. The lane led to open fields past the orchard that Andrew had showed them where some apples were on the ground.

'Look,' Ronald said suddenly, 'over there,' and to their surprise saw three pigs foraging in the grass. 'They must love apples, look how they scoff them down and what a noise they make.' Anne exclaimed. They also saw two bee hives in the orchard but did not venture near them. Beyond the orchard they could see some cows and horses in the open fields. They went into a field to see the cows, remembering to close the gate behind them. The cows moved quickly towards the children, who became nervous and stated to run to the gate closely followed by the cows. Frightened, they managed to climb over the gate before the cows reached them. They did not stop to see the horses but out of breath, ran straight back to the house. Uncle Walter laughed when they told him what had happened at supper that evening. He said the cows would not do them any harm, they just wanted to be fed but the children did not venture near them on their own again.

The following day Andrew came to invite them to meet his mother, Mrs Clayton, at their cottage. Anne said how much they would like to meet Andrew's mother and his brother Patrick who aunty had said was twelve, the same age as herself, Beth could not wait to see their cottage, she had heard so much about it. With Pip barking at their heels they walked up the lane to 'Higher Lydacott Farm'. Mrs Clayton was in the garden and as she waved to them Beth could see Andrew looked like his mother who smiled and seemed very jolly as she invited them into her cottage. Her curly fair hair bounced around her face and like aunt Rose she was a homely, rounded lady with a fresh complexion and rosy cheeks. Around her ample waist she wore an apron and on her feet she wore black laced boots.

Mrs Clayton seemed quite flustered. She made no apology for the state of the room but said, 'Do sit down.' Her home was very untidy with papers and clothes on every chair, not a bit like auntie's tidy house but Beth liked Mrs Clayton very much and the homely feeling of the cottage. As she gave them some tea, clucking chickens ran in and out of the room as Mrs Clayton asked them about themselves and if they thought they would enjoy living on a farm. As she spoke a big white cat jumped onto her lap and her tea spilt all over the floor. The girls managed to stop themselves from laughing at such an amusing sight. At that moment Patrick came in with his sheep dog Sabre and was surprised to see the girls and Ronald sitting among the confusion. He was a tall handsome lad, well-built but looked serious and reserved, not a bit like his brother s jovial personality.

'This is my son Patrick,' said Mrs Clayton to the girls.

'Hello, I didn't know you were coming today,' he said looking at his mother and commanding his dog to sit.

'Hello, I'm Anne and this is my sister Beth and brother Ronald,' Anne said smiling awkwardly. Patrick looked more mature than Andrew although he was only two years older.

Before Patrick could reply, Andrew said 'We could not find you to tell you.' Andrew knew he would like to have been at home when the girls came to visit.

'Nice to meet you,' he said, looking embarrassed.

Beth could see Anne particularly liked him as she smiled. 'We can't wait to explore uncle's farm and its surroundings, I expect we shall see you there,' Anne said shyly.

'I'm always busy on the farm but will be glad to show you around when I'm free,' replied Patrick picking up something from the floor.

They were to learn later that Patrick was embarrassed by the state the cottage was in. He knew his mother well. Beth imagined he thought they had come from a very well run house in Croydon. If only he knew how wrong his assumption was and how fortunate he was to have such a comfortable home. The girls enjoyed being in Mrs Clayton's company, she was very jolly and talkative and was known to be a good cook. They enjoyed having tea with her and loved especially her homemade scones and Devonshire cream and hoped they could call and see her again. After tea Andrew and Patrick took them around the cottage and soon it was time to say goodbye to Mrs Clayton. With Pip and Sabre barking excitedly at their heels the lads walked back to the farm with them. 'Goodbye, see you soon,' said Andrew cheerfully. Patrick smiled uneasily and said goodnight. When they were in their bedroom that evening, Beth was keen to ask Anne her thoughts about their visit to Mrs Clayton. Anne had noticed Patrick's reaction » when he saw them there but liked him all the same. 'If Patrick was told in advance of our visit, it would not have been such a surprise to him. I can understand his feelings. I thought the house was in a mess,' she replied.

Anne liked everything to be clean and tidy but Beth's thoughts were of Mrs Clayton and how pleasant she was and that was more important to her, after all

she must be a very capable lady. She not only had her home to run but also the ' livestock and garden whilst her husband worked on uncle's farm. Beth could hardly sleep for excitement. She could not believe how lucky they were to have the chance to live on a real farm. She thought about her school ^ friends and wondered where they were and if they were as fortunate as she was. The house was still and quiet. The fear of a siren going or bombs dropping on them was almost forgotten as Beth finally fell asleep.

Chapter 3
School Days

When Mr Bale was not so busy with his chores he often found time to take the children around the farm, especially to where they were told not to venture on their own. They went to count the cattle to see if any had strayed from the field. With his faithful collies Sheep and Honey by his side and to the amusement of the children, uncle Walter whistled his command and the dogs ran from one side of the field to the other, driving the cattle towards them. The dogs must be so intelligent, thought Beth, to be trained like that. After the cows were counted, uncle wanted them to be taken to another field to graze. So with the help of Sheep and Honey, the children enjoyed helping drive the cows along the lane. They had picked up a twig, copying uncle who had his stick and soon got the hang of tapping the cow's rump or tapping the ground calling out cow, cow, to help them on their way. They also began to learn some of their names. Beth had a favourite cow that was lightly coloured and called Blossom. Uncle said she was expecting a calf in the spring.

The time came when the children were preparing to go to school. It was their first term at their new school in the nearby village of Fremington. The school was at the bottom of the hill about a mile away from the farm. Uniforms were not necessary so their mother was thankful that she did not have to worry about buying them special clothes. Mrs Mayfield always dressed Anne and Beth alike and they were often taken as twins. On the first day to their delight, they were taken to school by horse and cart. It was great fun but they were told it was a special treat and they would have to walk back after school as the horse was needed on the farm. Their mother said she would meet them half way as it was a straight road from the school gate to the farm so they could find their way home quite easily.

Opposite the school was a small church and churchyard. The churchyard was to become a favourite place to visit as their teacher would take the children there for art lessons. Beth enjoyed drawing and painting and hoped one day she would be as good an artist as her mother was. Mrs Mayfield painted beautiful water colours when she was young. Below the church was a stream that ran under a little stone bridge where the children would throw a paper boat or stick into the water and watch it come out the other side to disappear as the stream meandered on its way. It was whilst playing by the bridge one day that the children were surprised by some marching soldiers who waved to them. They were told they were from an army base in Fremington.

The school had only one large room partitioned down the centre, one side was for girls and the other for boys. Each child had a wooden desk with an inkwell in it. A very big blackboard was at the far end of the room. In front of this was their teacher's desk and on it was a brass hand bell that was rung at break and home time. At the back of the school was the playground and at the front gate on a wooden platform were some milk churns and hanging on a chain on each was a ladle. When it was time for morning break the children would queue to have their mugs filled with milk. This seemed very strange to the girls after having milk in bottles at their old school. The school had a cat. It was a large tubby black and white cat and Beth thought that he must have drunk what was left in the milk churns, to make him so big. Beth also thought he was very spoilt because he was allowed to do whatever he liked, even sleeping on the teacher's desk.

Their first lesson was about the countryside. The girls felt sure it was especially given for their benefit. They were also told not to frighten the animals. They began to miss their old school friends as everything felt strange to them. The boys at this school were always up to tricks, far worse than those at their old school. They would put soap on the school door knobs making them difficult to open and crawly things in the girls' desks. When children did something wrong they were made to stand in the corner of the room until the teacher said they could sit down. The boys never seemed to get caught. Sometimes the teacher would forget that the child was standing there. When Beth was caught talking one day she forgot all about her, which made it an unfair punishment because her legs ached so much. The children were teased because they spoke differently and were called names. They were named the evacuee kids. However they soon made friends and in time could eventually understand the Devonshire accent.

On the way home their mother asked them about their first day at school. They did not mention the boys but explained that they were told about all the different birds that could be found in that part of the country.

'It might be fun to see how many we could spot going home,' suggested mother, trying to make their long walk home up the hill more bearable. The journey never got easier, for Ronald especially, when they had to walk both ways. He did not mind when it had been raining because water ran down the sides of the hill like a stream. He enjoyed walking in it on the way home, only to get into trouble when he arrived there. Soon after this happened a cane was attached to the wall above the breakfast table. Aunty called it her 'hot stick' however she never used it but glanced up at it when someone misbehaved or took it down and sat on it and that was enough of a threat. She was not to know their father had used a belt to discipline them.

The following day was Beth's eleventh birthday and she was very proud when Aunt Rose told her that her birthday was a special day, as it marked the first day of the farmers' year, which is the twenty-ninth of September; Michaelmas Day and farmers' New Year's Day. 'Perhaps 1 was meant to be on a farm,' Beth thought for she was happy and content and could not imagine a better place to live. After school Beth was surprised to see Patrick and Andrew waiting at the farm gate.

'Happy birthday Beth, Mrs Bale asked us over for tea,' said Patrick opening the gate for her and Anne who was walking a little way behind. Andrew also wished Beth a happy birthday.

'Oh, thank you, 1 didn't know 1 was going to have a special birthday tea party.' replied Beth, feeling very grown up. Anne smiled and said it was a secret.

As they entered the house a chorus of 'Happy birthday to you,' filled the room and on the table aunty and mother had prepared a delicious tea. In the centre was a birthday cake that aunty had made. Uncle gave her a hug. It was something her father never did. At that moment Beth could not have felt happier.

The days went quickly by. Andrew and Patrick often came to see the family and were happy to continue explaining the running of the farm to them. They all became good friends. Patrick did not join them as often as

Andrew as he was older and was kept busy on the farm. Beth often caught a glimpse of him and wished she was allowed to help him.

The days grew shorter by December and much less work could be done on the farm, although the daily rounds went on. All the animals were in their stalls. Anne and Beth helped to take their food to them and helped with other chores which they enjoyed doing. They thought how cold it was when one morning they found it had been snowing hard all night. From their window they could see that everything was covered in snow. The stone walls and trees and barns looked a perfect picture. They went downstairs to auntie's warm kitchen. Visible outside were uncle's foot prints in the snow. Sheep's and Honey's were there too. The girls felt sorry for their uncle who had to battle against the weather everyday but loved him for the way he cheerfully carried on as normal without complaint. Not a bit like their father, Beth thought, who was always grumpy. The girls did not talk about their father very often as they did not feel close to him, not as they did their uncle Walter whom they had grown to love. Beth asked aunty if uncle was lonely being away from the house most of the day. She remarked that he had the animals to talk to and seemed to be happily in touch with all living creatures. 'His thoughts may be elsewhere but he is focused on what has to be done,' she said cheerfully.

Aunty went on to say that their thoughts would soon be about Christmas as there was a lot of preparation to be done. It was one of the busiest times of the year. A great many chickens, turkeys and geese which they reared had been fattened ready for market. Some went to the market live but some were prepared at the farm! There were so many birds plucked for the table that Mrs Clayton had to be called upon to help. Uncle had been fattening some of the pigs for marketing too. 'He is very proud of his pigs,' aunty said looking amused as she knew he also enjoyed a piece of pork and crackling.

Three strays

Chapter 4
Christmas Joy

The children had broken up from school for their Christmas holiday and were glad because the school was freezing in winter. Aunt Rose said they could join her and mother on their next trip to Barnstable market. It was to be an exciting time as their mother had promised them that when all the produce was sold, they could go into town to do some Christmas shopping. Aunty had said that market days were even busier in December as not only the livestock was to be sold but also extra poultry and dairy produce that had been prepared and was needed for Christmas.

There was no worry about the weather as everything in the market was under a glass roof. The market stalls were very colourful and were draped with Christmas cloths and decorations and everyone was very busy setting up their wares for sale but Anne and Beth were allowed to wander and explore. Anne liked the pretty sets of china with thatched cottages and flowers painted on them. Beth admired the decorative horse shoes that had different painted flower designs on them. Aunt Rose bought the girls and Ronald a wicker basket each, that could be used on the farm to collect eggs or mushrooms, as well as many other things. The baskets were hand crafted and were in three different shapes so that the children would know which one belonged to each of them.

The following day the girls and their brother made some paper decorations for the very large Christmas tree that uncle and Derek had cut down and put in the 'best' room. The best (drawing) room was rarely visited, the sun being regarded as an enemy to be kept at bay with lace curtains. Mother helped the children to wrap the gifts they had bought and put them under the tree. The best room was situated at the front of the house and kept for special occasions. The room was beautifully decorated with holly, berries and mistletoe from the farm. It was a very exciting time for them all and like no other they had experienced before.

On Christmas Eve the people from the farm cottages came to visit them. Uncle gave them a joint of beef or pork for Christmas, a traditional custom, Derek with his wife Valerie also came, with Patrick and Andrew they brought uncle a brace of pheasants. Uncle greeted them and handed them some cider as they gathered near the open fire. There was such a happy atmosphere, something they rarely experienced in the past. Everyone had a merry time. Patrick and Andrew and the girls exchanged gifts to be left under the Christmas tree for the morning. As the merriment began, momentarily the war was forgotten. 'Shall we sing some carols,' asked uncle, as he looked over to Derek, 'did you bring your old squeeze box with you,' he said with a wink. Derek nodded and produced a piano accordion and began to play. Mince pies and sausage rolls were passed around as uncle roasted some chestnuts on the fire. Everyone enjoyed themselves and the evening drew to a close, the visitors left with shouts of happy Christmas to one and all. The children had never known a Christmas Eve like this one, of course they believed in Father Christmas, especially Ronald. Stockings were hung on the old stone mantelpiece and it was not long before they were tucked up in their beds.

In the morning they found that Father Christmas had left a bag of sweets, an apple and some nuts among games, comics and colouring books for them. The boys had bought Beth a book on modern farming and Anne was given a book about the countryside while Ronald had a book on horses. They were happy with their gifts and looked forward to their 'after dinner' present which was always a surprise. Mother gave them an after dinner gift as it was the custom that her mother had when she was a child. Beth was given a rag doll that had a ticket on it that read 'Lambeth Girl' from her father. She was told it was named after a well known song that was popular at that time called 'The Lambeth Walk. 'Their father was not able to come to see them that first Christmas, but the children did not mind, in fact, they were happy he wasn't there as they were frightened he may have spoilt it for them all because his moods were unpredictable.

Aunt Rose said they should all go to church before they had their Christmas dinner. It was not long before they were all ready in their Sunday best clothes. Mother looked especially attractive in a new dress with her long dark hair swept back into a neat bun. The girls hardly recognised the men when they saw them; they were also dressed in their best suits. Uncle looked so different to the children who were so used to seeing him in his old dungarees that were held up with a wide leather belt, jumper, waistcoat and his old trilby hat. Beth and Anne thought Andrew and Patrick looked handsome and mother echoed their thoughts by saying. 'The lads have grown into two fine looking young men. 'The boys looked embarrassed, as Patrick asked if they would all like a lift in his father's car and that they should all get there in two trips.

They thanked him and said they were pleased to accept his kind offer as it was a long walk on a very cold day. Whilst in the car the girls and lads thanked each other for their Christmas gifts. Andrew was pleased with his warm scarf and Patrick with his gloves, that mother thought would be an ideal gift for them at this time of year. Beth could not help but notice they were both wearing them that day. They were soon on their way to the little church that lay opposite the school at the bottom of the hill.

When they arrived, the church was almost full and looked especially nice, decorated with holly, berries and flowers. The girls could not have felt happier as they sang Christmas carols and wished those times would last forever. As soon as they arrived back at the farm the men changed and went out to feed the animals, while aunty and mother prepared Christmas dinner.

'A farmer's work is never done,' said aunty, as she saw Beth looking out the window at uncle crossing the yard, bracing himself against the bitter cold wind. Most winter evenings on the farm were cosy and special. The gas lamps were ht whilst uncle would feed the fire with logs as they sat and watched the flames flicker in the hearth and the smoke curl up into the chimney. Uncle would fall asleep in his comfy chair with Sheep and Honey at his side. Some chestnuts were in the hearth waiting to be roasted, something he liked to do when they were in season. Sometimes Aunt Rose and mother would do some knitting or embroidery or read a book. The girls often did a jigsaw puzzle or played cards with them. They never forgot the quietness of the room and the globed gas-mantle that kept making popping sounds. Aunty would turn the gas-jet down low before turning it up again to stop the popping.

The festive season soon passed. The weather was cold and wet and the days were short but there was still plenty to do on the farm which seemed to be well planned. Beside the need for Swedes and kale for the cows, one of the hardest jobs uncle said, was cutting marigolds for the winter food. It was cold, back aching work as the marigolds were cut low to the ground and then stacked at the edge of the field to be transported to the barn where they were sliced in the mangold machine ready for the cows to eat.

One morning Beth awoke very early and went down stairs to find uncle Walter getting ready to milk the cows. She asked to go with him and he agreed but told her to wrap up warm, as it was a dark, cold and wet winter morning. Uncle went out early in the mornings just as it was getting light, to milk the cows. He did this twice a day, every day. Uncle's lantern provided the only light inside the cowshed. As they entered they could hear the cows puffing and scrambling as they were disturbed from their rest. The cows were standing waiting in their stalls.
Harry, uncle's farmhand, joined them wheeling in a barrow of mixed feed, 'I see we have a new helper,' he said with a smile. He and uncle fed the cows and then began to milk them. 'They are so used to human company that you soon get to know them as individuals.' explained Harry, not knowing the children already had their favourites.

The following day, uncle explained that another hard job was muck spreading. 'Muck of course is animal manure, which is treasured and managed as carefully as any crop. The fields are spread with manure prior to ploughing. We are going out later this morning if you girls want to help but it is a very dirty and smelly job,' he warned. It was not long before they were putting on their Wellingtons and water proofs and joined Derek at the yard in front of the stables. The muck, or dung as it was known, was kept in a big heap in a huge ditch in the centre of the stable yard.

What fun they had loading the dung onto the cart, they could hardly lift their feet out of the muck. The manure itself was pretty slushy and the girls were getting it all over them but the dirtiest part was when the horse and cart was led from the dung heap to the field and back again. The cart wheels made deep ruts on both sides of the track and the horse's feet made deep holes in the middle. The ruts soon filled with muddy water and every time the horse put its hoof in the holes, he sprayed it all over them. The mud oozed over the top of their wellies and they laughed when they got stuck and had to be pulled out. The dung was put in heaps on the field to be spread later.

When they had finished the girls arrived back at the house, their mother and aunty laughed at the sight that was before them. Holding their noses they brought in the tin bath from the scullery and filled it with hot water in front of the fire. Although the girls did not smell very nice, they didn't mind as they had great fun. Ronald was upset that he was not allowed to go as he listened to what the girls had done. This was a new experience for the sisters, one that they never forgot. They especially enjoyed the bath by the fire as this was in contrast to their freezing drafty bathroom at home.

One day uncle and Derek were going to tidy up the hedges and said the girls and Ronald could go over to see them as they were going to light a bonfire. 'Why do you have to tidy up the hedges,' asked Ronald who was always asking questions. 'We have to cut away the dead wood and the remains of last year's growth, to give the hedge a chance to grow,' explained uncle. Beth had noticed there were hedges around all the fields. 'The hedges keep the animals from straying and eating crops which are not meant for them,' he continued. Uncle also reminded them that the hedges also provided a home for many birds and small mammals. Uncle wanted them to learn all they could about the countryside while they were still on the farm. It was a cold day and a bonfire, they thought, would be fun and was just what was needed to keep them warm.

The men left to start work on the hedges and later aunty made some sandwiches and a hot drink for the girls and Ronald to take over to them. They looked cold when they arrived and were glad of auntie's hot tea. The men had gathered up some dead wood, wild roses and brambles and it was not long before a fire was burning and the men warmed themselves and ate their food. As they watched the fire crackle with flames that lit up the sky, it reminded the girls of home on bonfire night. The only difference was there were no fireworks or their friends to share their new experience.

By the end of February the days were getting a little longer and everyone felt that spring was not far away. Aunty explained that every farmer welcomes the spring as the winds dry up the fields and allows the plough to get to work preparing the seed beds. 'Farmers usually plan well ahead so as not to use the same piece of field two years running; it is the best way of keeping the land fertile. Not only are wheat and oats grown but grass seeds are also sown for hay or making new pasture,' she explained. In fact aunty never tired of explaining the running of the farm to them.

Two years had passed since the family arrived at the farm and the war continued. Beth had learnt how their daily food depended on the success of the crops and a farmer's daily care. If the soil was poor they would not get a good harvest and much depended on the weather conditions too. The land on the farm must have been producing food for hundreds of years thought Beth. She had been told how the farmer has to look after the soil to keep it in good condition for the future. She wondered if she might be one of the next generation of farmers to enjoy working on the land. She thought it was not the possession of a farm that mattered. A farm seemed to Beth to be indestructible, something that could be enjoyed. She loved working with animals and now she witnessed the changing seasons and the fruits of one's labour, Beth felt this would be an ideal way to live and could not imagine living in a town again. That night she found herself thinking of Patrick, for whom she had developed a special feeling. She imagined herself older and being by his side, working on the farm together and wondered if he especially liked her.

Winter rescue

Chapter 5
The Promise of Spring

March arrived at last bringing longer days but there was a cold easterly wind blowing across the fields. One evening Derek came over to the house to say that Blossom had given birth to a calf, as she had done every year about this time. Uncle hurriedly put on his coat and said Beth could go with him as Blossom was her favourite and everyone else could see the calf tomorrow as too many people might distress her. Derek said the cow and calf were doing well. As they crossed the yard to the cowshed their lanterns gave a soft yellow glow which could be seen from quite a distance. Beth was the first to enter the cowshed and as she put her finger in the round hole of the wooden door to lift the latch on the inside, she experienced the warm smell of cattle and heard shuffles about the straw. Her heart felt as if it would melt when she saw the little calf.

'She has big brown eyes like yours Beth so we shall call her Betsy,' said uncle smiling at her. Beth thought what a perfect, wonderful day it had been.

Beth was so excited when they arrived back at the house, she wanted to tell everyone about Betsy but they were listening to the wireless. They sat quietly waiting to hear some good news but were told things were not getting any better at home. As soon as the news was over, Beth started to tell them about Betsy but her mother looked so downcast, worrying about her brother who was serving in the *RAF* and the plight her parents in Croydon, that Beth did not continue. Her grandparents were in danger of being bombed, living on the outskirts of London. Mother also worried about the food shortages there, as well as other hardships the girls knew nothing about. How could they have known then that one day they too would suffer the same experience when they returned home to Croydon.

As the weeks went by the thoughts of returning home were forgotten, with the excitement of discovering more amazing things happening on the farm. The girls were returning from school when they saw Patrick waiting for them as they entered the yard. He had come to see if they would like to go and see Betsy and help feed the newly born calves.

'Betsy and the other calves are getting stronger and one has just been born,' he explained. Patrick knew they would be excited to see them. They arrived just in time to see the little calf struggle to get to its feet, with its mother licking it all over at the same time.

'Oh how wonderful, 'Anne cried. 'I'm going to call it Anna,' he said smiling at Anne. 'I have never had anything named with me in mind,' exclaimed Anne showing her delight as she gently touched its head. Beth felt a pang of jealousy, not because of the calf being named after her sister but because of the attention Patrick was showing her.

Patrick showed the girls how to put their fingers in the warm milk and then into the calves mouth, so that the calves could begin to suck the milk from them, encouraging the calves to drink from the pail. He explained that they are really strong especially where food is concerned and although they have only just been born they would soon be happily drinking for themselves. Patrick went on to say that things didn't always go right for the calves.

'We lost a young calf yesterday, it had a twisted gut. It came as quite a shock to find her lying there dead having been perfectly alright the night before,' he explained.

Beth and Anne were sad and shaken when they heard about the calf but Beth thought she should not be so sensitive and must try to get used to hearing things like that, if she wanted to work and live on a farm. Patrick seemed always busy helping his father run the farm. Beth liked to help him when she could and grew to like his gentle ways.

'We have some more piglets if you would like to see them,' said Patrick, interrupting her thoughts.

The girls said they would and as they got near the sty, could hear pigs snuffling in their troughs and Ronald, who was already there, talking to them. He was very excited and asked Patrick where their mother had gone. 'She is in the next sty to prevent her overlaying on her offspring. Crushing under sows is a common way of losing piglets. She will be let in to feed them when someone is here to look after them. By June they will be fully weaned,' explained Patrick.

'Soon the pigs and piglets will be let out in the orchard all day. They enjoy rooting for apples and lying in the shade. They know that is good for them as pigs easily get sunburnt, which is very painful,' continued Patrick.

The girls could see he had work to do so they said goodbye and went to the stables to see the horses. As they arrived, they noticed the harness and tackle up on the walls and the cobwebs covering the windows. Beth laughed, as she suddenly remembered what uncle had told them. Anne had the same thought and laughed too. He said that some horsemen claim that if cobwebs were removed from the stables, the horses would catch cold. Harry was in there brushing down Gypsy

'1 have just finished here and the horses are ready to go out. Bramble is already in the field. Would you like to ride on Gypsy, Anne? Beth can ride on Paddy and Ronald can ride on Bramble, 1 will take you over and come back for your brother and sister,' said Harry, as he helped Anne up on to Gypsy's back. Beth waited as she watched them walk towards the field. She thought how marvellous it was to have the chance to be with the horses, something she had only dreamt of when she lived in Croydon. Ronald was getting excited too, especially at the prospect of riding on one of uncle's best hunters.

Harry was soon back and as he led the other horses out, he smiled and said that Ronald would make a good jockey one day. Anne was waiting by the gate for them.

'The horses like to be let out in the spring just like the cows after being in their stalls most of the winter,' explained Harry. As soon as the horses were let loose and the gate closed, they galloped and neighed with delight, sometimes rolling in the fresh green grass. It was a real change for them after being kept in and given mostly hay and oats during the winter.

The children loved seeing the horses enjoying their freedom. They thanked Harry for the ride and said goodbye. Walking back to the house Ronald said he was surprised when Harry told him that horses went to sleep standing up. The girls laughed as he ran ahead of them to the house. Outside the scullery door was a big water butt without a cover on it. Ronald ran over to it and stood on a large stone to look inside. The girls followed him to see what he was looking at.

'I can't see, help me up,' he demanded.

Anne lifted him up when suddenly he overbalanced head first and fell in. Beth screamed. Mother and aunty came running out of the scullery and grabbed Ronald by his legs and together pulled him out. He was coughing and crying at the same time. Mother and aunty were cross and upset as they took him inside. Then turning to the girls, 'What if we had not been here, your brother could have drowned you should have been looking after him. It is a good job your father isn't here,' cried mother who was in shock.

They were all sent to bed early that night and every night for the rest of the week and were warned not to go near the butt again. Beth is not sure to this day if Anne pushed her brother in on purpose, he was being so tiresome that day. She was not to know how serious the outcome could have been.

The following day Anne and Beth decided to go out for a long walk on their own. They were admiring the scenery when in the distance they saw a cottage hidden among some trees and went to see if anyone lived there. As they came nearer to the cottage, they stumbled onto a path that looked wild as if left to nature. They went down the path where the hawthorn hedges were laden with mayflowers. A post stood by an old broken gate with 'Little wood Farm' on it. As the girls came closer to the cottage they could see it was run down and in need of repair.

'Who could possibly live here?' queried Anne.

'I don't think we should go any further,' Beth replied feeling very uneasy.

Just at that moment a boy's voice called out. 'Who are you? I have not seen you before. 'A boy of about fifteen stood by the front door. He was obviously surprised to see them. He was round and podgy with curly fair hair and rosy chubby cheeks.

'We have come from Lydacott farm, 'Beth said not quite knowing what to

say. 'You are living with Mr and Mrs Bale then,' he said.

'Yes we are evacuees from London, we were just going for a walk, admiring the view and saw your cottage,' explained Anne. At that moment they heard someone calling from inside. 'Who are you talking to Richard?' said a woman's voice.

'It's two girls from Lydacott, mother,' he replied.

'Well, tell them to come in,' she shouted. Richard pointed the way and they went with him into the cottage. 'I'm in the kitchen,' she called. They followed Richard and there with her hands in a mixing bowl was his mother. She was as big and round as he was.

'I'm Mrs Higgins and this is my only son Richard. His father died in an accident on the Bale's farm so Mr Bale allows us to stay on in the cottage,' she explained.

'What is there to eat mother?' interrupted Richard before the girls could reply.

'He likes his food and I like to cook it for him. Anyone who marries my son will have to be a good cook' his mother said, smiling at the girls.

Anne and Beth looked at each other and tried not to laugh. Anne looked at Richard who was eating a huge bun and thought. 'I hope she is not thinking of us!' Mrs Higgins went on talking about how Richard was a blessing to her and when they could get a word in, the girls said how sorry they were and did not mean to trespass. She assured them she did not mind and said they must call again and get to know her son. As they left they noticed Richard was still eating and with his mouth still full, waved them goodbye.

The girls didn't dare to speak until they were out of sight of the cottage. They looked at each other still amused at what they had seen and burst into laughter, giggling all the way home. They could not wait to tell everyone about their adventure. That evening the girls told their story. Uncle said Mr Higgins was a good man and a hard worker and after his accident, he felt sorry for his widow and son. He said he would hire someone to repair the cottage for them, something he had been meaning to do for some time. Aunty said with a smile, that the girls should be careful as Mrs Higgins was looking for a future wife for Richard and teased Beth mercilessly about Richard many times after that day. Richard often came to visit them and one evening Aunty said to him. 'Why don't you take Beth to see the glow-worms?' Beth was so embarrassed that she hid herself away until he had gone.

Chapter 6
The Surprise

One morning Uncle Walter told the girls he had something special to show them, something that would surprise them over at the cattle shed. He told them to wrap up warm and explained on the way that he welcomed the cold breezes because they dried the wet sticky fields and allowed the ploughs to get to work preparing the land for the seed.

'Here we are. You are about to see a great sight, 1 have decided that because the cattle have been yarded under cover for about six months now it is time to let them loose. The cows had been looking over the gate for several weeks, that is a sign they are eager to be let out,' explained uncle. 'Watch them when they come out into the meadow, the grass has grown enough for the cows to go and have their first feed of fresh spring grass. They are happy to be out in the warm sunshine and onto the meadow grass after such a long time,' he continued.

He wanted Anne and Beth to see the cattle when they were let free, for it was a sight that still gave him pleasure. The girls were eager to see the cows when they were released and remembered what Harry had said when he let the horses out, that the cows enjoyed being let out as much as the horses. The cows smelt the fresh air and galloped out of the yard and tore down the field, frisking around, almost dancing before settling down to feed. Uncle thought they would be interested to know and explained that cows, sheep and other grass eating animals have complicated stomachs.

After swallowing the grass they bring back a mouthful at a time and chew it with great pleasure. It would be very useful if we humans could do that, wouldn't it, you could snatch a meal and eat it later when you had time,' he said and they all began to laugh.

It was an amazing and exciting moment for them to see the cattle come out like that. The children thanked their uncle and said they had enjoyed seeing the cows enjoying themselves after being let free. Beth thought they had so much to tell their friends at home.

As the weeks passed, planting continued throughout the spring and the work on the farm seemed to get busier. As soon as one crop was put in, it was time to put in another. One morning uncle said he was going to make some lambing pens ready for the ewes. Once the ewes were in the pens lambing started in earnest. 'There is plenty of grass around for them this year,' said uncle. The farm was busy day and night. Uncle and Harry had to visit the sheep many times especially after dark, to see if the ewes and new born lambs were alright. Derek and a farmhand helped take a turn during the day.

'The sheep dogs are a blessing at this time. They know just what the men want of them. The dogs almost take over by themselves and they are so gentle with the lambs,' explained aunty. There were about fifteen births a day and the weather was good.

'Keeping the right lambs with the right ewes and getting them to suck is not easy and the lambs on average seem to be noticeably bigger this year,' she continued. The girls watched as the outdoor sheep that were carrying twins or triplets were brought in and put in their pens. Two huge lambs died in the process of delivery but uncle did a marvellous job in managing to save the ewe. The ewe made a rapid recovery and was able to take a couple of triplets. Uncle said it was a hectic but rewarding four days during which 93 ewes gave birth.

One day uncle was on his way home when he picked up a half eaten lamb from the field. He thought it must have been a fox that attacked it. 'Maybe the fox had cubs to feed,' he said philosophically.

Uncle went on to explain that he did not have much trouble with foxes, just a few lambs and the odd dead calf now and then, although they also had taken chickens when they had been accidentally left out at night. Beth imagined it was never a pleasant thing to find a dead animal but it seemed to be an accepted part of a farmer's life.

It was an exciting time for the girls and Ronald as there were not only lambs being born, a lot was happening around the farm yard. There were young creatures everywhere; young piglets were heard squealing from the farm gate as well as the lambs that were heard bleating. Aunty also had some fine chicks and turkeys and some fluffy yellow goslings. Often a piglet or chicks and lambs would be brought to the hearth for warmth or to be fed. The girls enjoyed taking turns to feed the lambs with a bottle of milk. The lambs sucked so strongly from the teat that they almost pulled the bottle from their hands. They did not know what a comfort these memories would be then, in desperate times ahead.

Aunty would say uncle was very knowledgeable about his animals and was almost as good as a vet, who he sometimes called upon. He often brought a calf, foal or lamb with complications into the world.

The weather became mild as the weeks passed and the birds were singing when the girls, to their joy, came across a small area of woodland. 'This must be the place where uncle said he gathered wood for the fire and posts that he needed on the farm,' said Anne. They remembered that uncle also said that pea and bean sticks can also be found and that it saved him buying them at the market. They stood in wonder at the sight that was before them.

'How wonderful, a field of beautiful daffodils, don't they look lovely and so bright in the sunlight. Let us go back and collect our baskets,' said Beth. They raced back to the house and before long they were picking the daffodils to take back to their mother.

'They smell so fresh,' exclaimed Anne as they stood looking at the vast amount of flowers. It was a view, far removed from the town where they lived and the thought of ever leaving was too much to take in. They had come to love living in the country and on the farm. It was not only peaceful but interesting and so full of surprises. When they arrived back at the house their mother was feeding the wild cats outside the scullery door. She was delighted to see the lovely daffodils and as they handed her their baskets, she remarked on how healthy the girls both looked now, with their rosy cheeks and happy smiles. 'Coming here to live has done you both good, you look so well,' said mother wistfully, taking the flowers inside.

The girls thought mother looked well too. She had put on some weight. Beth remembered aunty had remarked on how painfully thin mother looked when she first arrived at Lydacott farm. 'I'm sure mother went without food so that we had enough to eat when we lived with father.' Anne said sadly.

There were so many cats around the house and as they were not house cats they did not have names. Uncle said they had their dudes catching mice in the ricks and barns. The girls often saw them on the roofs, out-houses too lying in the sun. [t was just another part of farm life, Beth thought. Mother came out with their ;empty baskets and asked them if they would like to collect some eggs with her from the hen houses and perhaps find some around the barns.

'Some chickens lay their eggs in the most unexpected and awkward places as they wander freely about the farm,' she said.

The girls carefully put the eggs in their baskets, some were white and others were all shades of brown. Anne noticed that some were dirty with feathers stuck on them. A few hens were still sitting in their nest boxes, so mother collected some eggs from them for hatching. The girls noticed she put them in a tray and took them back to the house to keep warm. 'Won't it be lovely to see the little chicks when they hatch,' Beth said excitedly, as they left the hen-house to look for more eggs.

The following day after breakfast Andrew came to see them with Patrick. 'My father is sheep dipping today, would you like to come and see the sheep being dipped? 1 have Pip here if we need him,' said Andrew.

'Yes, thank you, 'Anne replied. They all agreed that they would like to go but wondered what he meant as they had not seen sheep being dipped before. Soon they found themselves in a different part of the farm. They turned into a lane sheltered by some tall elm trees, then through a gate into a big field where a flock of sheep were noisily bleating and baaing.

They were met by the boys' father, 'hello there, 1 hope my sons are looking after you,' he said cheerily and pointing to some sheep he continued, 'they are going to have a special bath, come and see.' Ronald asked if sheep liked having a bath. 'Not really but it is good for them,' said Derek. Mr Clayton said they were to call him Derek, as everyone else did. Derek looked a lot like Patrick. He was tall and broad with a handsome face and dark eyes unlike Andrew who had fair-hair and blue eyes.

They all stood behind a fence and watched uncle and Harry, who looked after the animals, drive the sheep along as Derek dipped the sheep in their special bath. 'The bath is very smelly and they look so thin and white,' said Anne pitifully

'There are many good reasons why they have their wool clipped off,' Patrick explained, taking a caring interest in his new friend.

'1 wish you could have seen them before being shorn, I'm sure they were happy to shed such a heavy coat in this hot weather,' continued Andrew.

Harry drove the sheep along between two fences and Derek picked them up by their front legs and lowered them into the specially made pool. Uncle, to their dismay, poked the sheep under with a long pole until they were thoroughly wet. 'They almost drowned, 'Anne whispered.

Harry, with the aid of his collies who kept control of the sheep, allowed them to run out and join the others in the field. The girls thought it was cruel and didn't think the sheep looked very happy but uncle explained that the bath or 'dip' as he called it was for their own good, keeping them free from infection especially after being shorn. After watching the sheep all morning the girls laughed at the fuss they had made. There were so many things they still had to learn about the animals and country ways. As they all walked back to the farm Patrick mentioned to the girls that he and Andrew would be going back to school soon. They both attended an all boys' school in Bideford. It was Patrick's last term now that he had turned fifteen. He said that uncle wanted him to continue working on the farm and he would do so for as long as he was needed. Anne, who was also fifteen, said she would be helping aunty, until she returned to Croydon where she would have to find work. Beth felt sad, as she could see that things were going to change, they were all growing up and Life would not be as carefree as they had known and loved.

They all arrived back at the house and entered by the scullery door, as they knew they should leave their muddy boots there. Their wet coats could also hang inside, as the warmth from the kitchen would soon dry them. 'Come on in and warm yourselves, while I make you all a hot drink,' came auntie's welcoming voice from the kitchen. All thoughts of change were forgotten as they huddled around the fire and in the knowledge that they would all be friends forever.

Chapter 7
Hay Making

One morning Ronald woke Beth early by jumping on her bed. 'Wake up Beth, wake up, they are going to start haymaking. Derek and Patrick are outside with the tractor, if you hurry they might give us a ride.' The sisters hurried with dressing and Beth hoped that her brother would not get into too much trouble.

' Directly after breakfast they ran out to the hayfield. Andrew and Patrick were there and gave them a wave. Ronald was first to ask Derek if he could climb on the tractor. 'You can get on but hold tight,' he said with a grin.

'Come on Beth,' shouted Ronald. She jumped up beside him thinking he would fall and knowing she must keep an eye on him.

'We're off' called Derek.

Andrew was watching them, 'Be careful, hold tight,' he cried running over to them. They tried to stop their teeth from chattering as the tractor roared and started to shake. It was not the comfortable ride that Beth had expected. It was a good thing they held on to each other. Derek was also jolted about in the driving seat but seemed to enjoy it. They could see that behind them the tractor was pulling a machine that cut the hay. It fell in a long row behind them. When the tractor stopped, Derek laughed. 'Did you enjoy that my boy?'

'That was great fun, thank you,' he replied smiling. As he jumped off "Andrew came up to Beth and asked her if she was alright and if they were not too shaken, would they like to see the shire-horses. Anne and Patrick were standing nearby. 'Let's all go after dinner,' said Patrick seeing Beth looking a bit peaky. They agreed that would be a good idea.

It was not long after dinner before they were out in the fields again and soon found Harry who was harnessing Hercules to a rake on iron wheels. They heard the sound of his jangling harness that shone in the sunlight and his occasional contented snort and the plod of his large feet as they went off" to gather the hay. Andrew and Patrick were waiting for them. Andrew handed Beth some carrots to put in her pocket. 'How nice of him,' she thought as they went over to see the other shire-horses.

'This is Beauty,' said Andrew. He was a huge horse with a long black main and lowered above them.

'Don't go near his legs,' said Patrick anxiously. Beth looked down at his great feathered legs and feet that were covered in red mud and thought the boys must know all the dangers on the farm, being brought up on one. Beauty was strong as well as gentle. Beth offered him some carrots which he scooped from the palm of her hand, just as Andrew had shown her. In the distance they heard Harry's voice calling 'come on old boy' as Hercules pulled the rake along the rows of cut hay. The girls could see that wild flowers were growing there. The rake was drawn up and down the field and when the curved prongs were full, Harry pulled a lever and the hay was dropped.

'Are you still enjoying living at the farm Beth, it must be over three years now' said Andrew who enjoyed being in Beth's company.

'Yes, very much, 1 would like to know all there is to know about farming and would like to live on a farm one day,' she replied. He could not have known what it was like for them in Croydon before they came to Lydacott farm, she thought. 'There is so much to do and see in the country and everyone has been so kind to us,' remarked Beth.

Andrew seemed happy at her reply. Beth secretly wanted to say, 'especially because you and Patrick are here.'

They all took a rest out of the sun under an old elm tree when they saw their mother and Aunt Rose coming toward them carrying baskets. 'We thought you might like a picnic, it is such a nice day,' said aunty waiting for their reaction.

Ronald was jumping up and down with excitement said. 'Oh yes please, 1 like picnics. 'Anne and Beth laughed as they knew Ronald was always eager where auntie's food was concerned. Harry was called to come and join them as Andrew and Patrick helped lay a blanket on the ground. Before long they were enjoying a tasty meal of ham, cheese and homemade bread, with mother and aunty joining in the meal.

After the women returned to the farm Anne asked Patrick, 'Why do they have to rake the hay?' Patrick, who had been picking some flowers for her replied, 'I'll show you,' he said and led her into the field. Andrew and Beth followed them.

'Touch the cut grass and sweet smelling clover now lying in the sun,' said Patrick. 'Why it's almost dry, 'Anne replied, it smells lovely. Andrew smiled at Beth and taking her hand laid it underneath the cut grass and turned it over. 'You see, where the heat of the sun has not reached it, the grass is still green and damp.' explained Andrew.

"you rake the dry grass to turn it over so that it gets dry, then it is called hay. All the rows will be turned by this evening and Harry and Hercules can take a well earned rest. Shall we go back now, I'm sure you must be tired too,' said Patrick thoughtfully. They all walked back to the farm making plans for the following day. When the girls went to bed that evening they talked about the things that had happened and with mixed feelings of Patrick's attention to Anne and thoughts of Andrew holding her hand, Beth fell asleep.

The next day was also exciting, for the hayricks began to take shape. Derek appeared again with the tractor and with cries of joy Ronald was allowed to climb up and hold the wheel. It was a very short ride before Ronald had to jump off as Derek had a lot of work to do. They watched as he drove down the field once again. On the front of the tractor was fixed a large machine with prongs on it, which pushed the dry hay in front of it as it moved along.

The girls noticed that there were women in uniform helping the farmhands in the field busy lifting hay with pitchforks. Uncle explained they were land army girls who had come to help with the war effort. Andrew was standing with uncle by a strange machine that was called an elevator. It carried the hay to the top and then dropped it on a hayrick. Beth and Anne were fascinated as they watched the hay being moved. Patrick was also helping with the hay. Derek came up with the tractor and they all started to build the hayrick. After a while Derek looked up at the sky telling everyone to hurry as it would rain before evening, so the girls lent a hand. What fun they had with uncle and some farmhands were at the bottom of a sort of 'moving staircase' tossing the hay onto it.

It was not long before Anne and Beth were suffering with scratched hands and arms which were aching as they picked up armfuls of hay. Patrick could see their plight and went over to them. 'I think you should take a rest now girls, you have done enough,' he said, quite concerned but Anne insisted she was alright and wanted to continue. Beth sat watching for some time. It seemed however hard the men and women worked, they never seemed to clear the pile of hay that Derek was making bigger all the while as he drove his tractor to and fro over the field, while Ronald was happily chasing rabbits.

Beth looked over and noticed Anne had stopped helping and was trying to suck a splinter out of her finger. The next moment Patrick was by her side. Beth was upset to think that both brothers seem to make a fuss of her. She knew Anne was pretty with long fair hair and blue eyes but she wondered why Andrew had not gone to her rescue. 'You are working too hard,' said Patrick as he took the splinter from Anne's finger. Beth thought to herself that Anne could have stopped work when she did. 'It's not fair Anne always gets everyone's attention,' she said to herself.

Beth must have looked unhappy as Andrew came up to her and said 'Shall we walk back now Beth, I think it is starting to rain.' Beth agreed as she hurriedly took Ronald's hand, her eyes full of tears.

Anne and Patrick followed and as they were just leaving, they heard uncle call out. 'Thank you everyone, you have all worked well today, I'll see you later.'

As the sun went behind a cloud it started to rain as they walked back to the farmhouse. The men and women carried on working until late into the evening and the hay was safely gathered in before sunset. When the girls went to bed early feeling very tired, Beth tentatively asked Anne who she preferred, Andrew or Patrick. She said she liked Patrick but Andrew had a great sense of humour and she found him easy to talk to. Beth replied that she did not particularly like boys and climbed into bed. Although Beth was tired she did not fall asleep immediately. She kept seeing Patrick holding her sister's hand and thinking how nice Andrew had been to her.

Chapter 8
Father's Visit

The weather had been warm and sunny and uncle had gone into the kitchen garden as he often did after finishing his day's work. The girls could not help noticing that he wore layers of clothes even in the hot weather. Aunt Rose said he always wore short sleeved vests, long-legged underpants, a thick flannel shirt, corduroy trousers, a waistcoat complete with watch and chain and a trilby hat. When asked if he found it rather hot with so many layers of clothes on, he would reply. 'Well I've always worn them all these years and I'm certainly not going to change now. Have you not heard the old saying, what keeps out the cold keeps out the heat'! No more was ever said on the subject.

Beth and Ronald had broken up for their summer holidays. Anne, now that she had left school, helped aunty and mother on the farm. Aunty had said that farmers hardly ever went on a holiday as they were much too busy and contented working on the farm. Ronald and the girls were very excited when their mother promised to take them on the bus to Westward Ho, a seaside village not too many miles away from Fremington. The day came when they arrived on the shore. The seagulls cried and wheeled overhead as they stood looking out to the sea. The sandy beach stretched out in front of them and it seemed as if you could walk out for miles before you reached the sea. What a joy it was to see the cliffs and rock pools. Ronald amused himself looking for crabs, while mother sat on the beach, content to read her book. Anne and Beth looked for different shells to collect. They spent many happy days there, while they were on their school holidays and it seemed so natural to them, as though they had never lived anywhere else.

One morning their mother surprised them saying their father was coming to visit them. Anne and Beth looked at each other knowing each other's thoughts and tried to look pleased. They did not have many happy memories of their father. In fact they were quite frightened of him. The children had not seen him for almost three years. On the other hand Ronald was happy at the thought of seeing him again. Mother smiled but Beth didn't think she looked happy When the day came for father's visit, Derek took them in his car to meet him at the station but Ronald stayed with aunty until they returned as there was not enough room in his car. The girls felt apprehensive and hardly a word was spoken on their journey to the station. They felt sure Derek must have wondered why, perhaps mother had told him about their past. They had become such good friends, in fact the girls had never seen mother so happy since they left their home in Croydon.

They were on the platform just before father's train arrived. As he greeted them there were no out stretched arms as he went towards mother to kiss her. The girls didn't think he had changed at all. He was tall and thin with fair hair and blue eyes, quite handsome in a rugged way. Beth clutched her sister's hand when she saw he was still wearing his leather snake-like belt. The belt was unmistakable in its design. It had two thicknesses of leather that were interwoven and the memory of it made them shudder. It was unusual to see him smiling so much as he talked to mother, it made his presence less foreboding. Mother introduced him to Derek which made her feel uneasy. Not a lot was said as they set off for the farm. Ronald was waiting by the farm gate and jumped in the car to the farmyard. He was very excited as he took father in to meet uncle and aunty. There was much news to catch up on over tea.

Father asked aunty if the children had been on their best behaviour and hoped they appreciated all that was being done for them. Aunt Rose showed him her 'hot stick' on the wall. He was not to know that she had never ever used it; he just presumed that she did. Anne and Beth were glad she did not tell him about Ronald and the water butt. Father stayed for five days, mostly spent with the men shooting rabbits on the farm. As he spent very little time with the children it seemed as if they were not there. Anne thought it was because they were not under his charge, as they had been in Croydon. In the evenings he spent his time smoking and talking to uncle about the war.

The girls felt a sense of relief when the time came for him to go back home. They knew they would not miss him as they had not seen him for such a long time, not that they were ever close. When they arrived at the station there were many men on the platform in uniform. Father kissed the girls for the first time as he said goodbye. Beth was sure it was to impress

Derek as there was no warmth in his embrace. He told mother not to hang about the station when he kissed her and jumped on to the train.

He called to mother from the window, 'I can't wait to get you home.' ^

They watched the train disappear in the steam from the engine. Anne and Beth hugged their mother, glad that he really had gone. They all stood there transfixed until the train was out of sight, worried that it might even come back. Derek gently put his arm around the girls and said, 'let us go home.'

That evening Beth overheard mother tell aunty that father was rather possessive, especially where other men were concerned. When the girls went to bed Beth old her sister what she had overheard. Anne replied, 'it was a good job father didn't hear the wolf whistles the RAF men gave mother on the bus, when we vent to Westward Ho.'

The girls did not sleep very soundly that night. They felt that their father had intruded into their world. It made them feel vulnerable once again and they ;:new their mother must have felt the same. If only they didn't have to go back but they knew it was inevitable one day. Anne and Beth decided they would try and not think about it until the time came for them to return. The following day mother said she would take them on a bus into town. 'I thought we all needed cheering up,' she said with a smile. It was Friday, Barnstable market day but Mr and Mrs Bale were not selling any of their produce that day so they told mother :o enjoy a free day with the children.

They enjoyed their time spent discovering parts of Barnstable's market town. \n old spire town clock stood in the centre and not far away the river Taw ran under an old stone bridge. Nearby was the train station. The local shops were quaint and not far from them was the glass-roofed open market. Every type of dairy produce and trade stands were on show. They saw spinning and weaving demonstrations. Animals outside in their pens were being auctioned and they listened while help was given to anyone tempted to try keeping livestock themselves. The girls saw some posters in the town about a forthcoming fete and children's fancy dress competition.

'Would you like to take part,' asked their mother.

'Oh, yes please,' said Ronald excitedly and the girls agreed although Anne bought she was getting a little old for that sort of thing, now that she had left school. What fun Beth thought, it was something they had not done before. The children talked about what they could dress up as on the way home.

Much of their summer holidays were spent amusing themselves on the farm when they couldn't find anything helpful to do. The day came when they took)art in the fancy dress competition. It was decided that Ronald and Beth would go as 'Jack and Jill' and Anne as 'Mary, Mary Quite Contrary' Beth enjoyed Dressing up but Ronald made such a fuss and was in tears and a temper as he did not want to put the sticky brown paper on his head. Mother had to bribe him with sweets but all went well in the end. They enjoyed taking part with the other children especially as they rode to the scene in a decorated horse and cart. Anne was overjoyed when she took first prize and Ronald and Beth came third. They were all given sweets as prizes but Anne was also given a certificate that she was very proud of. They were never to forget those carefree days that were their happiest. Those days, although they did not know it then, became a comfort to them in the future.

One evening Anne and Beth were in the old barn sitting on the swing when they noticed some bats hanging upside down on the rafters. Some were busy flying around outside. 'I hope they don't get into my hair,' said Anne.

'1 don't think they will do that, they are too busy catching insects. Do you remember our teacher telling us that in the summer there are plenty of insects about for them to feed on and that they hibernate in the winter,' Beth replied trying to take her sister's mind off her hair.

At supper they spoke to uncle about the bats. 'Do many bats survive the winter?'Anne asked.

'If the bat hasn't stored enough fat during the summer months of plenty, it is unlikely to survive prolonged cold weather. They like being in the barn as it is well protected and draught free,' explained Uncle.

'Do be careful when you go in the barn won't you, your uncle keeps lots of old tools there. Tools that ought to be in a museum,' aunty continued. Uncle gave the girls a wink and asked if they had heard the barn owl hooting, as if to change the subject. The girls replied they had often heard its call.

The following day uncle invited Anne and Beth to go to the blacksmith's with him. Harry was going to help with the horses. Eagerly the girl's said they would like to go. The blacksmith's was not far from the school at the bottom of the hill. Beth sat on Bramble and Anne was on Gipsy as they left the farm. They were amused to hear uncle and Harry's horse talk. Whoa, gee-up and all sorts of commands and phrases telling the horse to go or turn. Sometimes their accent became an unintelligible sound. Uncle never shouted at the horses or whipped them.

'Blacksmiths are a wonderful lot of folk, their work is back breaking but they are always cheerful,' he said. 'At the blacksmiths you can always catch up on the latest gossip, people come and go bringing in news from their part of the country,' explained Harry.

Soon they came to the old forge and as they led the horses into the cobbled stone yard, the girls saw an old man sitting, working a pair of bellows. It was quite a sight to see the fire blazing and the smoke rising. The blacksmith came and measured the horses for shoes. They had been shod many times before and had developed a trust with the blacksmith so didn't mind going to him to be shod. It looked a painful operation but the girls were assured that the horses did not feel a thing. Uncle told them that the old man was the blacksmith's father and their family history went back many generations. When the horses had been shod, they said farewell and returned home. Uncle said the horses knew their way back to the stables themselves, without being guided. Beth thought how intelligent they were.

Now that the girls were older they were given many more chores to do. One was to pump the water into the water trough for the animals. It stood beside the water butt in the courtyard. It was hard work and made their arms ache. They enjoyed watching the cows pause to drink there as they came back from the field for milking. They would patiently wait in turn before slowly moving along their way to the milking shed. Just like the horses, they did not have to be led, they knew where they had to go. Beth especially liked to feed the chickens, the movement of their heads always made her laugh when they clucked and pecked for food around her feet.

The daily routine continued as usual, until one unforgettable day when Beth was with her mother in the kitchen. They heard a knock at the front door. It was unusual in that everyone came to the side door of the house. A telegram boy was there and he handed mother a telegram. As she opened it Beth saw her hand tremble. He asked her 'will there be any reply madam?' 'No thank you,' mother murmured and they went inside. She sat down by the fire, looking very upset and began to cry. Beth went over to comfort her and she explained that her younger brother Fred had been killed whilst serving with the RAF. Suddenly it seemed that the war had touched them personally for the first time. Anne and Beth began to realise how fortunate they were as life on the farm continued safely, while not so far away England was still at war.

Beth thought of the telegram boy and wondered how he managed to get past the geese and ducks in the lane as uncle had said they didn't like intruders. He also explained that the geese were happy when they had plenty of space and liked pottering around the farmyard and didn't like to be disturbed. They lived in a wire run at the top of the garden. Beth had often seen Harry washing down the concrete floor and putting in a new bed of straw for them. The girls liked to help aunty put out cooked vegetables and soaked bread for the geese and ducks but she said they must be careful not to leave stale food lying about when they fed them, as that would attract rats. The ducks and geese were very destructive and messy but aunty didn't seem to mind. One day the girls had collected some duck eggs for her and she remarked on how useful the eggs were for cooking. 'They can be fried or you can make excellent cakes with them,' she said with a smile, knowing how much the girls enjoyed her pastry and cakes and it was not long before she taught them to do the same.

Opposite the garden, down a well trodden path and covered in ivy was the outside toilet. There always seemed to be a goose on guard when Beth went near it. She thought they knew she did not like them. It was a chemical toilet with a large wooden seat, that aunty scrubbed clean so much that it was almost white. It was not a nice place to visit in the winter or any time when it was raining but the girls soon got used to their trips there.

Ronald enjoyed seeing the rabbits hopping about the farm. Derek said they were a big problem because they graze and devastate large areas of crops. The girls thought it was a pity as they were so cute but it didn't stop them from enjoying auntie's nice rabbit pies and stews. There were also plenty of chickens in and around the yard that reminded the girls of how horrified they were when they saw their mother and aunty killing the chickens and plucking them for the first time and preparing them for market. Feathers were flying everywhere, everything was covered in them. They could not bear to watch the feathers being plucked or hear the ripping sound as they did so or see the neck dangling over their mother's knee. How could their genteel mother do that? To make the deed worse aunty gave Ronald a chicken foot and showed him how to make the claws move by pulling a tendon. He enjoyed this immensely, especially when making a clucking sound and chasing his sisters with it around the farm.

Chapter 9
Barnstable Market

One day aunt Rose asked the girls to help in the dairy as she and mother were going to prepare for market day. The dairy was a very cold place to work in and they hoped they would not have to stay there very long. Aunty kept the dairy immaculately clean, as butter, cream and cheese were produced there from the milk that uncle had brought in from milking. Aunty explained that it had to be cooled and strained. It was put in a barrel butter-churn that stood on a wooden stand. Mother explained that when you turn the handle attached to its side, the tumbling motion helped to set the butter. 'Look through the small eye glass, that s where you can see the progress of the butter before the churn is opened,' she ;aid and suggested that the girls should each take a turn at the handle. Anne and 3eth just managed to turn it but found it very hard to do and were pleased to 3e given other things to try.

They learnt that the 'whey' was drained off to be used later as buttermilk or **pig** food. They watched aunty wash the butter in water and pat it into shape with wooden pats which then left a serrated pattern on the rich golden blocks and rolls of butter. Anne thought they looked too nice to eat, as their mouths began to water at the thought of it. Their mother asked the girls if they would like to weigh them. They both tried but were not very good at it so they were asked to wash the eggs and put them in boxes instead, which they did, albeit very slowly n fear of dropping them. It was very quiet in the dairy but for the eerie tap, tap, tap on the window pane from a branch in the wind outside.

It was Friday, market day at Barnstable. All the dairy produce had been packed ready to be loaded onto the cart. Uncle and his helpers had left the farm much earlier that morning with livestock he wanted to sell to buy new stock, especially I knew bull to strengthen the strain of his herd. Later Derek and Andrew brought :he horse and cart in the yard and helped aunty and mother load the dairy produce, vegetables and fruit onto it. It was not long before they were all on their way The town was always packed on market day and as they got nearer they could hear the noise of people shouting, calling and talking. Dogs were heard barking among other animal noises as they got close to the covered market which was easily recognised by its ornamental Victorian ironwork and glass roof. All the stall holders seem to know each other as they occupied the same stands **as** they had always done for many years. The whole scene was full of colour and activity. Aunty explained it was not only a market but a place for the village and farm folk to meet and catch up on the latest gossip. Mother enjoyed helping to sell the produce she had helped to make. It was in stark contrast to her existence back home in Croydon. Beth felt sure that like her, she did not want to return there either.

That night they all had plenty to talk about. Uncle was pleased with his new bull and asked everyone to think of a name for him. 'Well,' said mother with a smile, 'he made such a rumpus about getting out of the lorry, I think we should call him Rumpus. 'They all laughed and agreed that was a good name for him so Rumpus it was.

The girls were up early the next day still full of happy thoughts of their day at the market. Mother said the morning was a good time to pick some mushrooms for uncle's breakfast when he returned from milking. As they put on their wellies and coats Ronald joined them, as mother explained the dew was still on the grass and that was the best time to pick them. They soon found some hidden in the grass and put them in their baskets, Ronald pulled the tops off of his as he picked them leaving the stems in the ground. Uncle was pleased with our efforts and enjoyed them for his breakfast but the girls and Ronald didn't like them and preferred their cereal and eggs instead.

Uncle and aunty had cheerful personalities but seemed to enjoy a good moan about the weather, which Beth found out later, was hardly ever right for them. Uncle came from a long generation of farmers who loved their work and he would say 'There is no better way of learning a job than by doing it yourself.' They were very fond and proud of their farm which was a good thing mother said, as they seldom had a day away from it. Apart from keeping an eye on the weather, they had to see if the soil was right for planting seeds, if the corn was ready to cut or if the fattening stock was ready for market. Such a lot to be done but all aspects of their everyday Life they took in their stride.

As the days and weeks passed the girls came to realise that there was still much work to be completed on the farm. Mother and aunty were busy cooking everyday or making jam or bottling fruit. The apples in the orchard at the bottom of 'Lovers Lane' were getting larger and rosier daily. Some of the trees were so heavily laden they looked as if the boughs would break with the weight of the fruit hanging on them. Aunty said the children could eat as many windfalls as they liked. The picked apples would be going to the market to be sold. Anne and Beth thought they were the sweetest apples they had ever tasted. 'Sow Sow' their new pet pig, thought so too. The following day they saw the farm workers going 3n their way to the orchard with long ladders. They rushed out to join them. The girls enjoyed helping to the pick the apples that were on the lower branches. By lunch time, the trees were cleared. Anne and Beth were shown how to wrap and jack the apples into wooden boxes ready for Barnstable market.

Sow Sow with her favourite fruit

Chapter 10
Harvesting The Corn

It was not long before Beth and Ronald broke up for their school half-term holiday and then almost before they knew it uncle Walter told them, as the weather had improved, he was making plans to cut the first corn field. The following morning they were all up early and after breakfast went out to the field. Derek and his tractor appeared from the barn but the machine he pulled was very different from any others they had seen before. Derek said it was called a binder and explained to the girls that on its sides were wooden blades that revolved and bent down the standing corn on to knives that cut it.

Fascinated they watched the corn as it was carried into the machine, then it moved along and was tied into bundles which were thrown out at the other side, one after the other. Beth wished that her friends in Croydon could be there to watch it and wondered where they had been evacuated to and if they were staying with nice people. Perhaps they were on a farm somewhere in England, she hoped so as it was so much better than living in a town, she thought.

The girls enjoyed walking behind the binder but as soon as they saw uncle Walter they asked if they could help. He showed them how to stand the sheaves of corn upright in sets of six, standing three each side. The girls were not strong enough to do this for very long but it was fun watching the binder clacking around the field and to see the uncut golden square in the middle getting smaller and smaller until the rabbits that were hiding there, rushed out for the shelter of the hedges around the field. Everyone on the farm came out to help stand the sheaves upright including their mother and aunt Rose. This, the girls were told later was 'stooking.' In the distance Beth saw Andrew and Patrick also busy helping to stack the corn. The sky was getting dark that afternoon and as the cool breeze sprang up the girls were thinking they would make their way back and as if to echo their thoughts Derek appeared wiping the sweat off" his brow and called out.

'There is going to be a storm, you had better go back to the house, before the storm begins to break,' he said, looking at Ronald and the girls. Patrick and Andrew said they would go with them. Anne and Ronald didn't want to leave the field but aunty said they could make their own tea and look after themselves and they would join them later. This idea sent them all rushing back to the house. When they all reached the empty house, it was as dark as night. Patrick lit the gas mantles whilst Andrew put some logs on the fire. Through the windows they watched the storm for some time dramatically raging outside, forgetting about getting their tea. Suddenly they noticed aunty and mother with their heads covered with sacks looking wet through.

'Are we in time for tea?' said aunty smiling as they entered the room, looking at the empty table. 'Your uncle and the others will be here any moment.' The children looked sheepish as aunty and mother started to prepare the food. Everyone helped to set the table, feeling very hungry indeed. Uncle and the other workers came in wet and tired. The farmhands and land-army girls sat at the long table and it was not long before they were all enjoying hot soup and homemade bread, fruit scones, strawberry jam and cream, honey and auntie's golden buns which completed the scrumptious meal.

'This is what I call a real proper tea, not like mothers at home,' said Ronald, quickly stuffing another bun in his mouth. Ronald knew better behaviour at the table, as father would not allow the children to even talk whilst having a meal, but that was a long time ago and he had forgotten. Aunty gazed up at the hot stick, then took it down and sat on it. Anne and Beth looked at each other.

'How could he show us up like that in front of everyone, poor mother,' thought Beth looking at her sister who looked embarrassed. Patrick noticing the girls' awkwardness took everyone's attention as he turned to his father and said, 'How is Dazzler today? Is he settling down? I have not had a chance to look at him.'

'Who is Dazzler? Do tell us,' Ronald asked eagerly looking at Patrick.

'Why, he is our new hunter. Do you know what a hunter is?' asked Patrick, looking at Ronald, who shook his head. 'It's a horse which runs and jumps well and is used for hunting. Farmers hunt foxes to keep them from stealing poultry and killing sheep,' Patrick explained.

'Harry is looking after Dazzler with our other hunters, Paddy, Gipsy and Bramble. If you like I will get Harry to show you tomorrow,' uncle said and went on to explain that the ground was too wet to continue harvesting at the moment.

'I wish it was tomorrow already,' said Ronald who could not wait to see the horses. Anne and Beth felt the same. Tea was soon over. Beth felt very grown up being with the workers and everyone. Anne looked at Patrick and thought how kind he had been after their brother's outburst. The storm was over and it was getting dark as they said goodbye. Andrew called out, 'We will see you at the tables tomorrow,' and waved goodnight.

The following morning Ronald was excitedly rushing about the house, so ;ager to see the hunters. As Beth and Anne entered the kitchen, greeted by aunty who was waiting for them, she said, 'Uncle has not come back from milking yet lo would you like to come and help me bring in some vegetables from the garden for dinner,' looking at Ronald who looked disappointed. Before their brother could show his impatience at having to wait longer Anne said to him, 'Let's go and see who can pick the most.' They went outside and aunty explained how different vegetables grew and showed them how to pick them, she then put them n her trug. It was interesting to the girls as their mother normally bought them Tom the grocers, when they lived in Croydon.

Soon they heard the sound of uncle's hob-nail boots on the cobble stone yard and rushed out of the garden to meet him. He was not very tall but broad and muscular and he always carried a walking stick. Mother said that like many other farmers, long hours of hard work had made him very strong. He greeted them saying, 'Derek and the boys are already with the horses.' Looking at Ronald he said, 'Would any of you like to come and see Dazzler?' Seeing Ronald's eagerness, be often teased him.

They made their way over to the field gate where the horses were waiting. Patrick turned to Beth and introduced her to Dazzler. 'If you stroke him on the bead he will know you like him,' he said, smiling at her knowing she was a little nervous as Dazzler towered above her.

Beth was a little hesitant as she climbed the gate, he looked so big but the horse didn't seem to mind. She thought Dazzler was very special and felt strangely safe with Patrick near her. The girls knew Ronald would like to ride on him but uncle was quick to say he could when he was older. The girls and especially Donald enjoyed being with the horses and stayed until it was dinner time.

It was some days before they could enjoy the remains of the harvesting. Once again the farmhands and the land-army girls were there to help uncle and Derek with the corn. At last uncle said that all the corn could be stacked, having dried out quite nicely in the stooks. Once again Hercules, a big shire horse, was called upon to pull a low cart over the field. Slowly Hercules hauled it round, while the men and the women tossed the sheaves onto it with their pitchforks. The pile of sheaves grew higher and higher until the cart could take no more, then each load was taken to the edge of the field.

Over in the corner of the field the men were beginning to make a great stack. This was much bigger than the hayricks from the first early harvest that were in the field. Beth amused Ronald, running among the remaining stooks playing 'hide and seek' and had fun chasing the mice and rabbits that were hiding there. Their mother, aunty and Mrs Clayton brought refreshments over to the field and everyone stopped to eat and rest. The girls could see how hard the work was but no one seemed to complain. Beth thought if only she could stay on the farm forever, she would never be unhappy again.

By teatime the stacks were so high that ladders were put up against them so that the men could get down. Ronald wanted to climb up the ladder but was not allowed to. It was not long before the harvest was gathered in, with golden stacks each neatly thatched with roofs of straw and standing in rows along the edge of the field. Uncle and Derek looked very proud of them and thanked everyone for their hard work, 'Let's all go back to the house for supper. I'm sure the ladies have made something nice and nourishing for us to eat,' announced uncle. Everyone looked forward to Mrs Bale's suppers as she always put on a wholesome meal and so they soon made their way to the house knowing the weather had been kind and another year's good harvest had been brought in.

The girls enjoyed working alongside the land girls who, they were told, like them, had no experience of country life before coming to work on the farm. They planted, hoed and then gathered in every imaginable crop. There was much hilarity about muck spreading but they got on with the job as well as hay making, harvesting, including building corn ricks and thought it was a good life.

Chapter 11
Harvest Festival

The weeks passed and at supper one evening uncle looked at the girls and said. 'You have seen nearly everything that happens on a farm. Do you still want to be a farmer's wife Beth?'

'Oh yes, 1 have never been as happy as 1 have been living here. 1 love the animals and being on the farm, there is always something different happening every day and each season brings its own changes and interesting things, especially at spring time,' replied Beth enthusiastically.

'Well we have a lot to be thankful for, that's for sure and whilst we are talking about being thankful, it is time to think about the Church Harvest Festival,' aunty exclaimed.

It was not long before everyone was talking about the coming festival. Mother, aunty and Mrs Clayton met up with the village ladies with their produce to decorate the church for the service on Harvest Sunday. The little church looked beautiful with all the colours of the flowers, fruit, jars of jam and honey and vegetables. Aunt Rose made a large loaf with three fish decorated on it, to put on the altar. She looked very happy as everyone sang the hymn, 'All good gifts around us are sent from heaven above.' The harvest festival was a great morale **booster** for the land army girls. It was the one time of the year when they felt that "this is what it is all about." One girl even said, 'God does his part of course 3ut we plough the fields and scatter the seed on the land.' Each year they were invited to take part in the harvest festival service at the village church. Pews were reserved for them. The vicar would say a few words before he began the service, reminding everyone what a great pleasure it was to see them, "the wonderful working army (The Women's Land Army) ."After the service people gathered to eat and drink the tasty homemade refreshments. The girls were very proud of their mother and aunty who had worked tirelessly to make the service such a happy one, the memory of which was to stay with them for years to come. For the land army girls it was off home for their Sunday dinner feeling full of goodwill and patriotism.

Work on the farm continued. One day, Beth and Anne were in the courtyard when Patrick asked them if they would like to come and help him and his father drive the cattle back from the field for milking. The field was by a stream where ;he cows were leisurely eating grass. With Derek's good-natured dog Pip they
helped to drive them back to the farm. Patrick said that before very long there would not be enough grass in the fields for the cows and they would have to come in to be fed and it would not be until May before the cows began to sleep outside again. 'That will mean less manure to wheel from their stalls every day,' laughed Patrick smiling as they followed the herd into the cow shed.

The girls knew most of the cows by name and felt that they had come a long ' way from their first encounter when they ran away from them. They stopped to watch the milking when Derek suggested that Anne and Beth might like to try their hand at it. 'May 1 try and milk Blossom?' Beth asked wistfully.

'It is Blossom you should really ask but I'm sure she won't mind,' said Derek. 'You'd better use this empty pail for fear you might spill what's in mine. Now just do as I show you,' said Derek.

Somewhat gingerly, with Patrick at her side, Beth tried to follow Derek's instructions and although there was none of the regular squirt, squirt, squirt that she heard when Derek was milking, Beth managed to get a little frothy milk in the pail. 'That's a very good attempt,' said Andrew who was now standing in the doorway. 'We need a new dairymaid to help us, you had better ask Mrs Bale to put that in a bottle for you.' He said with a grin. Beth suddenly wished she was not there, being sensitive, she felt Andrew was laughing at her.

'Well done,' said Derek as it all went quiet, 'a little more practice and you will be as good as your mother.' Derek Liked mother, who enjoyed working with him, she was extremely attractive, not a bit like the women who worked on the farm, Beth thought to herself Although Andrew was only teasing Beth she was quite put out by his remarks.

'I'm quite proud of my first effort and I don't like you laughing at me,' said Beth looking sternly at Andrew.

'I think it's time for tea, there is no more we can do here today,' said Derek, sensing some tension between them. Beth lay awake that night thinking that it was not like Andrew to make fun of anyone. Perhaps she was imagining it: what must he think of her she thought, as she closed her eyes to sleep.

After school the next day Beth decided to go for a walk by herself. She thought of the special moments spent on the farm and how difficult it would be to return to Croydon when the war was over. Andrew and Patrick had become her close friends. She could not imagine not seeing them again. Her interest in farming had grown and she thought she would truly like to be a farmer's wife one day. Beth thought how farmers got to know their animals through spending time with them every day, some over many years. She remembered uncle explaining how difficult it was after being in close contact with the herd, to have his favourites taken away to the slaughter house; it was a hard wrench for him.

Living in a town would never be the same again. How will she bear it? The thought of living with her father and his cruel temper made her fearful of returning home. Everyone had been so kind to them since the day they arrived that Beth felt that they had always been like one family. The farm and surrounding area has been a haven for them all, with a freedom that was not possible in Croydon. Beth was beginning to feel downhearted as she walked along the path and heard the sheep bleating down the road in response to the silent, bright eyed collies. It was to be just one of the sights in her memory.

The weeks passed. The country was still at war when the family heard from their father that a bomb had dropped near their home and the house was unsafe to live in but he was able to find a suitable house to rent nearby for us. It was not long after this that the day came when England celebrated the end of the war. Then came the dreadful realization that the family would have to return to their new home, to live with their father again. Anne was now sixteen and would have to go to work when she returned. Beth was fourteen and a half and Ronald twelve and would have to finish school.

Chapter 12
Farewell Lydacott

On the 7th May, 1945 the end of war with Germany was being celebrated but Beth and the family remained on the farm for some months afterwards. One autumn morning their mother, uncle and aunty were sitting by the fire talking when Anne and Beth came into the room. There was uneasiness and a quiet atmosphere about the room and they wondered if something had happened. Aunty said they had something to tell them. The girls went over to the fire and sat down. Mother said sadly it was time for them all to return to Croydon, as their father wanted them to come home and was looking forward to seeing them again. Anne and Beth looked at each other and their hearts sank. It was not easy for mother to give them the news as she knew they looked on the farm as their home. Beth thought of Andrew and Patrick who had become such dear friends.

Uncle sat staring into the fire smoking his pipe. He dreaded this moment but it had to come. Aunty tried to look happy for them as she reminded the girls that their father was on his own and anxiously waiting for their return. How could she suspect that it was the thought of living with him again that was the cause of their distress and the fact that they could not bear to leave her and uncle and the farm. They had come to love them and see the family as their own. Their mother looked concerned as it was difficult for her too.

In their hearts they knew this day would come but going home would be like going to a foreign country. With the passing of the years and of the seasons their home had inevitably became Lydacott farm. They had come to love and appreciate country life, especially farming, the animals and the wildlife around them. They would miss their friends who they had grown close to over the years. It all seemed like a bad dream and they could not believe it was happening. Donald was upset to hear he was leaving and said he was not going. He could not bear the thought of leaving the farm, especially the horses.

Now that their father had found them a house, he could not wait for their return. To the children the news was devastating. Perhaps they could stay until Christmas but their hopes were dashed when they heard their mother making plans for their departure. Aunty Rose tried to console them by saying they could return in their summer holidays but she could see there was no way she could comfort them. It must have been difficult for her and uncle too, thought Beth.

'Aunty and your mother have become close friends over the years and she has grown to love you all as if you were her own as I have,' said uncle echoing Beth's thoughts.

'There have been good as well as difficult times living and working together but we would do the same again,' said aunty, with a lump in her throat. Things would not be quite the same again. The house would seem empty and quiet, she thought sadly, remembering the first time she saw the children and how they had filled her life, as if they were her own.

The girls went out to find Andrew and Patrick to tell them the news. They could see by their expression, that they had been told they were leaving and like them found it difficult to believe. 'You will come back and see us won't you,' said Patrick.

'Oh yes, we never wanted this day to come,' Beth replied, holding back her tears.

'We shall come back as soon as we can,' said Anne, putting her arm around Beth.

'Let's all go and see mother,' said Andrew, trying to relieve the situation. They entered the cottage to find Mrs Clayton knitting. When she saw the girls she quickly put her work aside. 'I can see by your faces, the time has come for you to leave us. We will all be sorry to see you go,' she said sadly.

'Thank you, Mrs Clayton we don't want to go, but aunty said we could come back, when we have our holidays,' cried Beth giving her a hug.

'Yes, we will all look forward to seeing you and the time will soon pass. You will be leaving school Beth and starting work and who knows what the future will bring,' she said looking at her, knowing that one day she would return.

The following day to make matters worse, uncle returned from the yard to say that Sow-Sow the family pet pig had died, everyone was sad to hear the news. 'Sometimes an animal will unexpectedly die but she was a good age,' he said, not liking to lose any animal.

'It did not seem that long ago when the children took it in turns to ride on her back,' thought aunty.

Uncle said he would give her a proper burial and suggested that the orchard would be a fitting place for her, as she had spent many of her days there. She was a very heavy pig, Derek and Harry had to be called upon to help uncle put her onto a wheelbarrow. Anne and Beth picked some flowers from the kitchen garden and they all walked down together to the orchard. The men dug a deep hole beside an old apple tree and lowered her gently into it. When she was buried the girls laid the flowers down on the grave and Ronald put a cross there that mother had made from some twigs. On returning to the house they felt that they had lost a dear friend.

It was the last night at the farm. Beth stood at her bedroom window. It seemed dark and empty out there and she suddenly felt lonely for the first time. Beth knew there was nothing out there to harm her but she felt vulnerable, the same feeling she had when her father came to visit them. The dark sky matched her mood as she climbed into bed. 'Things may not be as bad as you imagine Beth and aunty did say we were welcome to return at any time to see them, 'Anne said wistfully trying to comfort her sister. Beth could not reply, she closed her eyes in an attempt to stop her tears from flowing, holding on to the hope of returning to the farm she called home.

Sheep and Honey

Chapter 13
Returning Home

The day had arrived and they could not believe it was happening. It had all been so wonderful. It was a sad, bewildering moment on that cold winter's morning when they all said goodbye. On closing the gate Beth stood, eyes fixed on the farm and everything she had grown to love, as if to burn a picture in her mind, never to be forgotten. They had grown up healthy and strong there. They all hugged each other. Andrew hovered in the background until Beth gave him a wave and with his eyes fixed on her, waved back. Aunty, who held a hanky to her eyes, linked arms with uncle. Patrick stood looking dejected by the gate, as Derek started his engine to take them to the station. Beth felt her heart would break. She blamed her father for everything and resented the fact they had to leave those they loved and told herself it would not be forever.

It was a long time before the steam train reached its destination and pulled into West Croydon station and before they knew it they found themselves standing on a cold draughty platform with many other evacuees and soldiers returning home. Suddenly Beth was overwhelmed and totally lost. This was not where she wanted to be and from that moment Beth was determined never to stay in Croydon as she knew she could never be happy there.

Their father was on the platform waiting for them. He was pleased to see them and gave mother a hug and kissed her. He said that he had rented a house in Clarendon Road and that it was within walking distance from the station. As they walked to their new home Beth noticed the evidence of destruction everywhere. Some of the windows had been blown in at the terraced houses and the smell of burnt timbers among the debris still polluted the air. Not knowing what to expect they came to a sudden stop. 'Here we are,' father said as the family looked on in disbelief.

They stood outside a small terrace house with the name 'Why Worry' etched on a plaque, set in the brick wall between two bedroom windows. 'It would have been funny, if it were not so tragic,' thought Beth. Several roof tiles were lying on the pavement below. The house looked rundown and forlorn. There was no gate to the wooden fence and dirty, disintegrating curtains hung at the front windows. 'Come on in, I'll put the kettle on,' said father who must have sensed this family's disappointment at seeing the house.

Plaster had come down from the ceiling in the front passage as they went in. On entering the living room, father explained that the house had not been lived in for the duration of the war. They could not believe their eyes for the rooms were small and everywhere looked dark and gloomy. 'I was lucky to find this house. A lot of people have no roof over their heads because of this war. Most houses are unsafe to live in and those that are safe like this one, are in much need of repair and decoration,' continued father as he made them a hot drink.'1 will make up the fire and you will soon feel at home.'

'No way,' thought Beth as she looked at her sister, whose expression, echoed her thoughts.

They kept their coats on as the room felt so cold and damp. Their mother sat down and the girls could see she was distressed but they were too scared to say anything. The house with its dark green and brown paint work and damp walls must have been worse than she had imagined. After they had something to drink, father took Anne and Beth upstairs. The bare painted wooden stairs creaked beneath them as they went up to see their bedroom. There was lino on the floor. It had a double bed, a chest of drawers and a chair. 'I know it is not like the bedroom you are used to but I expect you will soon make it cosy for yourselves,' he said leaving the room.

As their father went down stairs the girls looked about the room in disbelief. They never imagined it would be like this. The net curtains were falling apart and dirty, hanging on a piece of string stretched across the window. The windows were almost black and the wall paper was peeling from the walls. Ronald came in to see their room and noticing the peeling paper, tore it down and to their horror bugs ran out all over the wall. Ronald squashed one and blood splashed everywhere. Anne screamed. 'Let us go and tell mother.' she cried.

'What's all this noise and screaming about?' demanded father as he entered the room.

'There are bugs on the wall,' shouted Ronald, 'we are going to tell mother.'

'You will do no such thing. You are not to worry her, they won't hurt you,' he demanded.

under the blankets, he went out and found his old heavy greatcoat and to their surprise put it over them. As they felt warmer, they eventually fell asleep. Beth dreamt she was on the farm and woke up disappointed to find herself not there. There were no familiar sights and sounds, only the gloom of the bedroom. Suddenly the room began to shake and the windows rattled as they heard a train go by. The girls jumped out of bed to see a thick blanket of smoke covering the garden. Dressing quickly they went downstairs to see Ronald looking out of the kitchen window. 'The train went through the bottom of the garden,' he shouted in sheer amazement. There was a wire fence between the garden and train lines but it was not noticeable in the haze of smoke.

Their mother, who was preparing breakfast, looked downcast and said, 'that is why the windows were black and curtains so dirty.' 'Oh, mother I cannot believe we have to stay here,' cried Anne who had hardly slept all night.

'I'm afraid this is our home now, it will take us a while to settle but we will manage,' mother replied trying to comfort her. 'Come and have your breakfast,' she continued while putting some toast on the table. Beth suddenly realized father was not there and asked where he was. 'Your father was up early this morning and has gone to Petticoat Lane, in London. He said he always went there on a Sunday morning,' said mother.

They were relieved he was not with them as they were full of questions to ask their mother but before they could speak they could see she was eager to speak to them, before their father came home. 'I know it is going to be difficult for all of us to adjust to life here but we must try and do our best to accept it. With your help we can soon clean up the house and in time I'm sure things will get better. It will not be the same as we have rationing and shortages here. That will mean we will not be enjoying fresh food and vegetables as we had on the farm but I will do my best to see that you will not go hungry,' said mother smiling a weak smile as she tried to explain the situation without upsetting them too much. They missed auntie's generous helpings of puddings, lamb stews, her lovely scones and Devonshire cream. Poor mother, Beth thought, she looked so despondent as she went on to explain that father had work at the moment but that

Without saying a word Anne and Beth took their brother down stairs. Mother had prepared some sandwiches for them. 'Come and have something to eat, I expect you are hungry,' she said unaware of what happened upstairs.

The bugs were to keep them company for a long time after that incident. Like most boys, Ronald didn't mind, he had fun squashing them. A small fire was glowing and they could feel the heat in the room and its warmth made them feel better" especially after having some food. It had been a long time since they had left Devon. Father said there were three bedrooms so Ronald could have his own room too. 'The toilet is outside but there is a bucket at the top of the stairs you can use at night,' said father.

A door from the kitchen led to the garden and the outside toilet. If it was raining you would get wet walking around the house to it. Also the toilet roof leaked so the floor was always wet. The light did not work so it was a good thing they did not go out at night. After hearing the bucket being used outside their bedroom door, the girls were embarrassed and managed to wait until morning. Cut-up squares of newspaper hung on a nail in the toilet, some had even fallen in the wet on the floor; the seat seemed always wet, not a bit like auntie's scrubbed wood top toilet. Beth felt disheartened as she tried to accept the fact that this would be the way they would live until she was old enough to leave. As she looked around her she could only see a grim picture of the future.

The girls hoped that after a night's rest they would see things in a better light in the morning. The bed clothes felt damp and cold as they climbed into bed. They cuddled up close together for warmth, when their father heard them talking and came into their room. He could see them shivering

might not always be the case, as times were hard and there was not enough work for everyone. 'Try and be good when your father comes home after work. He is not used to having children around him when he comes in after a heavy tiring day at the builders' yard,' she said anxiously. Ronald was too young to grasp the situation but Anne and Beth knew exactly what their mother meant. They had not forgotten what it was like before they were evacuated.

'Don't worry, mother, we will be good and try to stay out of father's way,' said Beth, trying to reassure her. They had felt protected in Devon from his moods and temper and now they were constantly trying to avoid his presence. He was quick to anger, which only added to the tension that everyone felt. Later they heard father's unmistakable steps coming towards the back door and when, he came in they could immediately tell by his expression that he was thankfully in a good mood.

'I have something for each of you,' he said, pulling some frocks out of an old carrier bag. Mother gave an awful sigh at the clothes and colours he had chosen. To gave her a frock with bright yellow flowers on it. They could see when she thanked him that it was one she would never wear. The girls also thanked him "or their frocks, looking as pleased as they could as their hearts sank to their shoes. Donald was given a jumper that he would soon grow into. 'I'm starving,' father aid, looking at mother. He sat down at his usual place at the head of the table, expecting to be waited on. He then turned to Anne and Beth. 'Go and help your mother in the kitchen and later you can help tidy up this room but don't make ınoise as I shall be going to bed for a couple of hours,' he continued.

He always went to bed after his Sunday dinner. The girls knew they had to keep quiet, they also knew from past experience not to speak at the table but Donald was too young to remember what life was like before they were evacuated, although the girls did warn him but he had forgotten. As the children at down with their father for dinner, Ronald started to talk about the train. Beth rose in her seat when she saw her father's hand come down and slapped him cross the back of the head.'"We want to eat our meal in peace, be quiet and keep our eyes on your plate until you are finished,' he demanded.

The girls could see tears well up in their brother's eyes but he did not cry, perhaps he was too numb with shock, they thought. All went silent; they were all too frightened to say anything. When their father went upstairs to bed, Beth heard Ronald whisper to his mother that he hated father. Their mother always made excuses for her husband and explained that when he was young, being the eldest son of ten siblings, he was severely disciplined by his father who was a policeman. He would be blamed for their wrong doing and would be punished severely for them. They, too, were also not allowed to talk at the table. Fortunately the girls and their brother did not share meals with father too often as they had their dinner at school and ate tea before he came home from work. That evening mother said they should have a bath. They had gas and electricity. A kitchen geyser managed to provide hot water. Along one side of the kitchen behind a plastic curtain that hung in front of it was a full sized bath. When they first pulled the curtain open the bath was full of green slimy, smelling water that must have been there before the war started. The girls did not want to use the bath even after it had been cleaned. How they yearned for the old tin bath in front of auntie's open fire. It was cold in the kitchen and their mother fit the gas oven to give out some warmth but there was always a cold draught that came from under the back door, so it did not really help. One day Beth was in the bath and Ronald bought he would pull a trick on her. He found a bag of muddy potatoes that were in the kitchen and opened the curtain and threw them in. Beth screamed as the muddy potatoes went down in the water, splashing over and around her She could hear her brother's laughter as he flew out into the garden. Mother came to the rescue and gave him a warning, that she would tell his father if he did it again and kept what he did a secret.

Monday was washing day and after the clothes were washed they would be put through the mangle and cranked one by one through its wooden rollers to wring out the excess water. It was a painful experience for Ronald when one day Beth accidentally caught his finger in it. A line was put over the bath to hang the washing on. There was a line in the garden but the washing suffered from the black smuts that came from the trains that went by several times a day. Mother only used the line when she had to. The washing always hung around the fire for days on a clothes horse or chair to dry and air. The fireplace was very small so there was a fight to get close enough to feel any warmth. It was not like the open fire on the farm that seemed to heat the whole room. They came to realize that this was the main source of heat for the whole house. Sometimes the chimney failed to draw properly and smoke bellowed out into the room when it was windy outside. Mother said the house was in a bad state of repair making the rooms cold, draughty and damp and what heat they were able to generate flew straight out of the broken doors and windows. As the bugs and spiders still lurked under the wall paper and curtains they all began to appreciate their home on the farm more than ever.

However, to the family's amazement father had a piano in the front room, it was a great surprise to them when they heard him playing it. He did not have any music but played by ear they were told by mother. He would pick up any tune and managed to play it using both hands. They enjoyed those moments when he played as he seemed like a different person. He would ask the girls to sing the latest songs, which they enjoyed doing so that he could play them eventually Beth found she had a good ear for music and could play like her father. Soon she found she could play a cheerful tune to lighten her mood or take out her frustration by thumping loudly on the keys. When feeling calm she played a pleasant melody but always when her father was not at home.

Chapter 14
Nitty Nora
Now that Anne had left school she needed to find employment and with mother's help managed to find work at Alders in Croydon, a large store in town, in the dress department. Anne had always taken an interest in fashion so was very happy to work there. It made a difference to her life as she was not only able to help mother with extra money but she could eventually save up to buy new clothes and shoes, of which Beth became very envious. Beth was to be in school uniform for another term. The school felt strange to her after being in one large classroom in Devon. The 'Croydon British Girls School' was a large building with many classrooms and corridors. Beth did not feel comfortable there. Her mother was also able to find Ronald a place in Christ Church junior school, near to their grandmother's house in Handcroft Road and within walking distance from their home.

The memories of Beth's other school were so ingrained on her mind she found she could not settle. She felt so awkward that she did not feel she belonged there. The children made fun of her Devonshire accent and she knew no one from the past. It was some time before Beth made friends but eventually she made a close friend, an Irish girl named Kathleen Keough. She came from a large I family and had seven brothers, four of whom were sets of twins. They were a very close religious family. Beth loved to visit their home, although Kathleen's father was strict they made her feel welcome and she felt at ease away from the tension that loomed at her house.

Beth's last term was one she would never forget, especially the day when Nitty Nora the flea explorer' as the children called her, came to the school. She was an austere looking woman, short and stout with her hair tightly tied back in a bun. She looked at the pupils' hair, one class at a time. There were so many children infested with lice that when she came to Beth's class she stopped looking at each individual and marched the whole class out of the school and down to the old ' gas works in Factory Lane, not far away from the school. She said that the problem was out of control and in order to attempt to cope with it Nitty Nora was allowed a room with help and facilities in the building to deal with the infestation. Beth felt miserable and humiliated as she stood in the queue, wondering what was going to happen to them and worst of all what would her father say. The

children were hustled through a doorway one by one, to a table where a rather scruffy looking woman stood. In front of her she had a large bowl of white paste and a brush. Each child had to go to her and she brushed the paste
onto their heads. She insisted, 'tell your mother to leave this on until morning and then you can wash it out. It will kill anything you have in your hair.' Reluctantly when it came to Beth's turn and before she could protest, not that she dared, Beth felt a cold wet hard brush going through her hair. It smelt so awful she felt sick and could hardly breathe.

Beth left the room and found herself outside in the cold. She ran home crying and ashamed, hoping no one would see her. Her head was cold and wet and when she reached the house she almost fell in through the door. Her mother stared at her in disbelief. 'What has happened?' she cried. It was not a scene she had to confront before. Beth blurted out all that happened to her. 'You have no lice in your hair, as you know I check every night. Come let me wash that stuff off before your father comes home,' said her mother hastily going into the kitchen to get ready. Mother was drying Beth's hair in front of the fire when her father returned.

'What is going on here, it's no time to be washing your hair. I want my tea, he said angrily'

His wife explained about the whole class having to be de-loused. 'Well, it won't happen again,' he shouted, where's the scissors?

'Oh, no George please don't cut her hair,' pleaded her mother, knowing Beth loved her long hair.

'Her hair is far too long, it's just asking for trouble,' he said still agitated and shouting at her and with that, he found a pair of scissors and in one swoop cut Beth's hair, just below her ears. 'I should have done that a long time ago, it will be easier to keep clean now,' he said throwing the scissors back into a drawer. Beth ran upstairs and collapsed on her bed and sobbed. 'Oh my hair, my hair, I hate him,' she cried. Beth thought in her despair, that she could not go back to school and would never be happy again. Her father's harsh voice could still be heard downstairs. 'My poor mother she has been so careful, it is not fair, it is not her fault what Nitty Nora did,' cried Beth to herself Her heart sank when she looked in the mirror. 'What will my friends say, they will laugh at me,' she moaned.

The following morning her mother said her hair would soon grow and it really didn't look too bad. It was a hopeless situation; there was nothing she could do about it and Beth had to go to school. She walked to school in a trance wondering what her class mates would say when they saw her. Her friend Kathleen was the first to notice when they met outside the school entrance. 'What happened, who cut your hair?' she said, not knowing what to say to her friend.

'Father, it was because of what Nitty Nora did,' said Beth her eyes full of tears.

'Don't cry Beth, your hair will soon grow again and lots of girls wear their hair short like that,' said Kathleen trying to comfort her. Beth was surprised no one else seemed to notice or if they did, they made no comment that her hair had been cut short. Kathleen was right, Beth thought, as she looked around her class room, she saw that most of the girls wore their hair short with a fringe, not that it made her feel any better. Beth was relieved that this was her last term and hoped her hair would grow before she looked for work. Beth had learnt to type and hoped to work in an office. Her mother said there were always vacancies for office work in the newspapers. How Beth longed for that day to come.

As time went by the house became more comfortable to live in or was it that they were getting used to it! However, their father always seemed to be showing his disapproval and mother was always trying to smooth things over after any upset. There was never any real argument as father had his way, no matter if he was in the right or not. He would raise his voice in anger, especially if he knew he was in the wrong, each word carried weight. He would swear and blaspheme 'Jesus Christ' or 'Jesus wept' before he shouted at anyone. This used to upset the girls as they knew it was not right. Aunty would have been angry if she had heard him.

The house always seemed to be overcrowded because of the small rooms and this did not help the situation as far as their father was concerned. He could not : get used to having children around him and soon sent them out to play, saying he wanted a bit of peace and quiet. Mother often sent them to visit their grandmother to see how she was or to see if she needed anything, especially when her husband was in one of his moods. Father, they had been given to understand by grandma, who did not have a good word to say about him, was a common cockney and mother was too good for him. Anne and Beth thought it strange that their mother, an educated genteel lady could fall in love with him. Mother said he was a tall and handsome man and different from all the other lads she knew at that time. With his blue eyes and fair hair, she had fallen for his charm and sense of humour. He was not the father the girls knew. How could he have changed so?

On Anne and Beth's dutiful visits to grandma, their grandma would tell them things about their father that mother would not have liked them to know and she would very rarely visit them at their house. 'Your mother was a fool to marry him. Her father and I warned her. He is not of our class. He is heartless and your mother lives in fear of him. He has humiliated and abused her. They knew this to be true but what could they do. The girls found themselves going out of their way to please him. Hardly a word exchanged between them, for fear of upsetting him. There was always an atmosphere and they craved to be part of a happy family again. They were a family but did not feel a happy, united one, not like they had been in Devon. However, there were happier times.

One such time was on a bitter cold afternoon when the family were all huddled round the fire. They were listening to a programme called' Dick Barton Special Agent.' It became a favourite serial after the war and although it was difficult to hear as the wireless set crackled and screeched especially at the very moment something exciting was about to happen, they listened to the end. Their father was due in from his first day at the chocolate factory. He usually came through the back door but this evening he knocked at the front. 'That will be your father, how strange, why has he come round that way?' queried mother, as she went to open the door.

Anne, Beth and Ronald could hear their parents whispering, as they came down the passage towards them. Their eyes opened wide when they saw their father wearing a white boiler-suit and stuck onto it were lots of pieces of chocolate. Beth studied his face, he was in good humour and said, 'well it's still good stuff to eat, help yourselves,' and they did. They picked the bits of chocolate off father's suit as if their lives depended on it. The best was yet to come as they found even larger pieces of chocolate in his pockets. It was a real treat because they could not afford to buy many sweets, especially not chocolates at that time.

Their father was reduced to taking any job he could find and money was tight but mother said he seemed to have enough money to buy Woodbine cigarettes and newspapers. There was never enough money and Beth and Ronald soon understood if they wanted any pocket money they would have to earn it themselves. In the town there was a street market called 'Surrey Street' where Ronald and Beth would ask the stall holders for empty wooden fruit boxes and drag them a mile home. They chopped the wood up and tied it into bundles, to sell it as fire wood. Croydon had quite a few big 'well to do' houses. They would tentatively knock at each house door and always seem to manage to sell every bundle. Beth could not remember if there was a real need for their firewood or if people were just kind of felt sorry for them. Sometimes they were given something to eat or drink or extra money over what they had asked for. It was bitterly cold when they went out to sell their wood but they did not mind, they were happy that they had some pocket money to spend. Beth and Ronald had discovered a little shop in the basement of a house in Derby Road, a road adjoining theirs. It was called 'The Dugout' and sold all manner of things including sweets and drinks, such as their favourite liquorice dips and humbugs and lemonade that was made and sold by the glass to be consumed on the premises.

Another enterprise was making a 'guy' for Guy Fawkes' night. Although Beth ;was practically a young lady she had to look after her brother. Beth had found an old pram to put the guy in and mother gave them some old clothes and they made a guy. Ronald helped Beth push it to West Croydon station where they stood waiting for the commuters to walk by. 'Penny for the guy,' they would call out, not forgetting their 'please' or 'thank you.' 'Please put a penny in the old 'man's hat. If not a penny a halfpenny will do. If not a halfpenny, God bless you,' was their cry. When they became too cold or tired they would go home excited, to count their takings to see how many fireworks they could buy for bonfire night. It was a time they could look back, with affection for each other.

They didn't worry about having new toys or clothes as none of their friends had those. The clothes were always handed down. Children had to make their own amusement, playing hop-scotch or marbles on the pavement outside their 'house but mostly they went to the Wandle Park to play, as it was at the bottom of their road and then over Pitlake Bridge. They were able to stay at the park for my length of time, as long as they were home before night-fall. There were no sheep peacefully grazing but to Beth it was the nearest she could get to the open 'fields of Devonshire. The river Wandle was reduced to a stream that ran through the park. It had weeping willow trees along its bank. The branches of the trees trailed in the water, but further downstream the water rippled over stones and weeds. Most of the children who played in the park took their jam-jars and fishing nets there to fish for sticklebacks.

Nearby, a wooden bridge went over the river which led to a hut that belonged the bowling green. Ronald and Beth could get into the hut when no one was about. It was their secret hiding place. Beth would day-dream and think of Patrick and of the day they had said goodbye. Patrick had stood motionless, as they left the farm. A moment before he had held Beth's hand saying 'be strong, it will not be forever.' It was the first time he had kissed her and she felt a closeness that must she thought, have meant something special. The hut became a haven, away for everyone, from their house and the impoverished streets that were all around them. Beth's thoughts turned to her father who said they were not to complain and that they were lucky to be alive and have a home to come to. What he said was true but his words did not give her any comfort.

It was not until sometime later that Beth learned that thousands of children were killed and injured by enemy action. Air-raid shelters had been built everywhere and blackout curtains were still visible in some houses. There were buildings without iron fences, the gates having been melted down for making munitions. Grandma had told them when the howling sirens went off, how everyone scrambled to the shelters in their gardens before the German bombs were dropped. She was hurt badly getting down into the Anderson shelter in her garden and was crippled for life.

One evening everyone was sitting around the fire and father had finished his dinner and was in a good mood. He amused the family by making animal shadows on the wall with his hands and fingers. They tried to do the same. Ronald thought it was great fun, suddenly they heard something scamper across the ceiling. Father said there were huge rats in the loft looking for food and they were to be careful to shut their bedroom doors at night. Mother said it was probably just a little mouse. Father said it was not a little mouse and there were not only rats up there but he was told the house was haunted. He was just about to continue when the windows rattled. Beth screamed. 'It is only the wind outside,' said mother and looking at the clock, said it was time for bed, thinking her husband had said enough for one evening. Beth was too frightened to sleep as every creak and knock haunted her imagination. What father had said kept going through her mind and then she was gripped with the awful fear that a rat would jump in her bed. She did eventually fall asleep and awoke with a sigh of relief that everything seemed to be the same. Mother tried to convince them that father had made up the story. However it was winter and the cold dark evenings seem to accentuate the eeriness of the night and they were still disturbed by it.

Mother had to 'make do and mend' and often there were holes in the soles of their shoes or plimsolls which were packed with cardboard to cover the holes in the bottom. As the cardboard got wet, the children wore holes in their socks which mother darned with whatever coloured wool she could find. This was embarrassing for Beth at school as it was hard to tell their original colour. Father put studs in their new shoes to make them last longer. Beth did not mind that as she could make a sound like a tap dancer.

Things began to get better when mother found work at an ornament shop near where they lived. The shop was one of a row in Handcroft Road that also happened to be near grandma's house. The shop sold plaster ornaments. The : owner supplied other shops and the fairground with them, for prizes when the fair came to 'Mitcham Common' twice a year. It was always a big order which •kept them busy most of the year round, as well as selling them in the shop. It was wet and dirty work for her pouring plaster into rubber moulds but the extra money meant that she could buy extra food and new shoes and clothes for the family, especially when their father was out of work. As grandma lived near the shop, sometimes mother was able to have dinner with her and catch up on family news, however mother had to suffer the wrath of grandma's tongue when she vexed her anger on hearing her husband's name. 'He is bone idle, laying in bed while you are out working I would throw a bucket of water over him if I was up there.' She exclaimed.

Grandma was very concerned when she heard that Anne had 'Scarlet Fever' and was taken to hospital. When the ambulance arrived Anne was taken down the stairs from her bedroom on a stretcher. Beth was so upset that she sat on the stairs and cried thinking her sister was going to die. It was a day the sisters never forgot. The thought of losing her was unbearable. She could not think of life without her but in time Anne recovered and there was great joy in the house when she returned home.

Chapter 15
Father's Fury

When the family got to know their neighbours they began to realize how lucky they were to have been evacuated. They heard harrowing stories of what the neighbours had experienced and the impact it had on them: the destruction by the bombs on buildings, their rooms collapsing all around them, 'it must have been terrifying,' thought Beth. The flying glass, people in shock and wounded, raging fires that were everywhere and the thick smoke and dust making it hard for people to breathe and the dreadful cry of people trapped and dying. It sounded terrible. They heard about the rescue workers and police doing all they could among the debris. At some point the 'all clear' had sounded, bringing a sense of relief among the desolation, as wreckage of their homes brought them to despair. Then with little sleep and exhaustion they wearily helped each other to clear away the rubble. Then came the realization that friends, neighbours and family had died and others by some miracle had survived. It was hard to believe this was all happening whilst they were living in peace and comfort in Devonshire.

  Beth recalled their father's mood changed when there was no work available. It was different when the war was on mother explained father was in work then and had no responsibilities in that his family were being cared for. Now they were a family again he was finding it hard to adjust. Beth thought he seemed to resent the fact they were happy and preferred their life on the farm and perhaps 'jealous of the affection they had developed for Mr and Mrs Bale, who treated them as if they were their own family. When they came home, their father scarcely knew them and they only had unhappy memories of him. They had all changed and grown apart and it was going to be difficult to bond again. Although their mother was with them, Beth felt alone, she missed Patrick and Andrew and everyone she knew.

  One day Ronald, oblivious to the fact that father was due home any moment and left to his own devices, while mother and Beth went out to fetch some fish and chips for father's dinner. Ronald with the fire poker in his hand played with the coal on the fire. 'Jesus Christ, what the hell are you doing?' father bellowed, raising his voice so loudly that Ronald dropped the poker in the fire. 'Oh, so you like playing with the coal, do you, well you can go and play in it,' he shouted and grabbing Ronald by the scruff of the neck, father opened the door of the coal cupboard under the stairs and threw him inside shutting and bolting the door behind him. Ronald cried hysterically to be let out, he said sorry, he would not do it again but father was not interested and harshly directed his wrath on their mother and Beth when they came home.

'Where do you think you've been and where's my dinner,' he demanded. Mother explained that they had just gone out to buy some fish and chips for him. Angrily, he said he found Ronald playing with the fire and the house could have been burnt to the ground. Mother didn't reply but looked toward the cupboard and put her hand to her mouth as if in shock, then she quickly put father's dinner on a plate and put it on the table. Father sat down and began to eat. They heard Ronald's whimpers from under the stairs. 'You be quiet or you will get worse than that, you will feel my belt across you,' he blurted out with his mouth full. Wide eyed and numb Beth listened to her brother's pitiful cries, whilst her mother sat with her eyes glued to the fire frightened to say or do anything that would aggravate the situation.

Eventually a sound from outside caused him to open the cupboard door. Fie pulled Ronald out and told him to vanish. He flew up stairs. 'Poor boy,' thought Beth who had never seen him so terrified before. It was Anne that they heard coming back from work and sensing something was wrong, asked what had happened., She had become bold since she had started work. 'None of your business,' father said, grabbing his coat as he went out banging the door behind him.

'What's upset him now?' asked Anne, looking at her mother who was still in shock. She explained to Anne what had happened.

'Ronald was playing with the poker, in the fire and your father came in and caught him and locked him in the coal cupboard.' Mother did not stop to explain anymore but rushed upstairs to Ronald who was still shaking and crying. Mother helped him to wash and stayed with him consoling him. Later she took him up some supper, saying he had better stay out of sight until tomorrow as when father was in one of his moods, there was no telling what he might do.

'The brute, I don't know how mother puts up with him. I'm going out, I can get something to eat later, I don't want to be here when he comes in. I might say something I will regret, 'Anne remarked, as she left the room.

When Anne had gone Beth sat and thought what their life could have been her mother had married someone else. At that moment her mother came in and sat by the fire with her. 'Will Ronald be alright?' asked Beth. 'He is quite shaken but he should be better tomorrow,' replied mother looking distressed. Later when Beth had gone to bed she listened for signs of her father's temper, sometimes he would hit her mother but there was no furniture being moved around or noise, only raised voices. Beth froze as she heard her father's footsteps coming up the stairs, passing her bedroom to his room followed by mother. Beth was thankful he did not enter Ronald's room. It was sometime later when Anne came home and Beth pretended to be asleep, she did not want to disturb her father by talking. Beth found she couldn't get to sleep, the night's events kept going through her mind. She was upset for Ronald, although he was in the wrong he did not deserve being locked in the cupboard like that.

The next morning Beth noticed her mother had been crying but nothing was said between them, only that Ronald was too upset to go to school. Beth thought she brightness disappeared from their lives, everything seemed grey. Beth didn't know what came over her, she felt depressed and she decided she must get away and before she knew it she was heading for the tram terminus. She had a three-penny piece in her pocket and soon found herself buying a ticket. 'We are going as far as 'Thornton Heath' said the ticket collector, giving her a penny change. Beth did not reply and it seemed a long journey before she heard his voice again.

'All change' Beth found herself standing on the pavement not knowing which way to go so she just walked until she found a wooden bench to sit on by an open screen.

Beth sat wondering what to do, with not enough money to return home and was beginning to feel cold when a policeman came up to her and asked her, as she was in school uniform, why she was not at school. Not knowing what to say, Beth did not reply. He then sat down beside her and asked her if she would like something hot to drink. Shivering Beth nodded her head and followed him in to the station. The bench was actually in their grounds outside the police station so Beth had been seen from the window. She was given a hot drink, before he asked for her name and address. Beth hesitated for a moment and then felt that she must tell him. He then asked her what had happened to make her want to run away. She told him about her brother and that she did not want to go back. It was explained to her that she was too young to be on her own and that her mother would be upset and worried if she did not return and it was his duty to take her safely home.

It was not long before they were knocking at the front door and her mother answered. She was at home with Ronald when normally she would have been at work. The officer explained what took place and asked if her mother was alright and said if she was worried about anything, he would stop and have a word with her husband. 'No, no that will not be necessary officer,' she assured him and after thanking him for his trouble, he walked away.

'Oh, Beth what made you do that, your father will be furious,' she cried.

'Do we have to tell him,' was Beth's immediate reply, frightened to know what he would do.

'We must tell your father or someone will and it will be the worse for us if we don't say anything. Did you not see the neighbours outside curious to know what is going on when they saw the police car? You had better have your tea and go to your room out of sight and I will tell him after he has had his tea. He may be in a better frame of mind after he has had something to eat,' explained her mother dreading the consequences.

It was not long before Beth heard raised voices downstairs, then her father's footsteps heavily rushing up the stairs, her door crashed open, he pulled Beth off the bed shouting that mother had just told him what she had done. He said Beth had shown the family up and heaven knows what the neighbours think and she had given her mother unnecessary worry. He took off his belt and hit her several times before her mother came in and tried to stop him. He pushed her away and went out swearing he would swing for them all before he was through. The next thing they heard was the front door slam shut.

The pain of the strap was not as bad as seeing her mother so upset. Beth said how sorry she was and that she would not run away again. Her mother said nothing as she gently bathed Beth's wounds. The buckle of his belt had cut into her skin. Beth stayed in her room and went to bed early thinking of Patrick. 'I will write to him tomorrow but will not tell him what happened today.' she thought. Anne came to bed after mother had told her what had happened. 'I'm sorry Beth, is there anything 1 can do?'

'No thank you, 1 will feel better tomorrow' Beth said miserably.

'Do you remember before we were evacuated, when we had gone to bed, we were not very old, when we were arguing about who was on who's side of the bed,' said Anne.

'Yes, I do, the bed-head had iron bars and we used to count them to find out exactly where the middle line of the bed was.' Beth replied.

'Yes that's right and we argued and pushed each other over on the right side of that imaginary fine, 'Anne continued with a smile. 'It was then whilst we were arguing, father came in and hit us with his belt for arguing and we barely had anything on, 'Anne said solemnly at the thought of it.

'1 shall never forget or forgive him,' replied Beth.

Anne, seeing her sister was getting upset again, went on to speak about their future hope of going to Devon for a holiday, before they finally fell asleep.

On the following Sunday morning their father returned from Petticoat Lane and without saying a word and to Beth's surprise, gave her a carrier bag. Beth felt inside and heard a faint cry. She could not believe her eyes, it was a dear little tortoiseshell kitten. 'Is it for me?' she cried.

He nodded his head and before Beth could thank him, he had walked away into another room. It was the first sign, she thought, that he might be sorry for what he had done, not that he ever said sorry. Beth was happy for the first time since leaving the farm. She grew to love the kitten as it was very special to her, t was her very own, something she could look forward to seeing when she came home and something that loved her too. It was so affectionate. Beth called her Fortie.

The children's relationship with their father continued to be difficult. His absence from them when they were evacuated did not affect them as it did him. Uncle Walter more than made up for their father not being with them. Uncle Iever hurt or frightened them, as he helped to bring them up. He taught them to care for and respect not only people but animals and everything around them. The girls often spoke of him with affection. 'He is such a character with his shirt sleeves rolled up to his elbows, his corduroy trousers held up both by braces and an old belt, 'Anne said cheerfully.

'I remember him gathering a tiny lamb in his great big hands, struggling to be fed and how we loved to feed them with a bottle beside the open fire,' continued Beth.

Life carried on as usual but they never went hungry. Their mother did all she could with what few ingredients she could buy. They ate a lot of fried food, there were bread-filled sausages, egg on fried bread, bubble and squeak (greens with potatoes mashed and fried) spam or corn beef that was disguised in more ways than one. Bread and dripping was a family favourite. Chips and mashed potatoes seemed to figure in most meals. They all enjoyed mother's vegetable pies and bread puddings, Ronald was always rummaging around for what remains were left over from the previous day. Beth never liked drinking her mother's weak tea made from dried reused leaves. Bread was rationed and meat allowance was just one shilling a week. There were not only serious shortages of food but clothes also. Mother often made the girls dresses. Beth was mostly dressed in pink, to go with her brown eyes while Anne had blue, to match her blue eyes.

She also made their coats from blankets, whilst grandma knitted them all jumpers and cardigans, gloves and scarves. Because everything was rationed mother had to encounter the dreadful queuing at the shops every day. How she must have longed to be back in Devonshire again.

Tortie

Chapter 16
The Letter

One morning, Beth, to her surprise received a letter, the first of many. She looked at the envelope and it was franked with the word Devonshire. Excitedly Beth took the letter to her bedroom and closed the door, her heart was pounding. She sat on her bed and quickly opened it and looked at the bottom of the page to see who had sent it. It said, with love. Patrick. Avidly she began to read it.

'Dear Beth, How are things going for you in Croydon? I do hope you are happy and settled with your family. I expect it was strange being there after living on the farm for so long. I am kept busy but I love the work, as you know. We all miss you and your family and it is not the same, 1 mean, not having you all around. We do hope you can come and visit us this summer. I understand you : will be leaving school. Do you know what you want to do Beth? Mr and Mrs Bale are keeping well and everyone sends their love and best wishes to you all. Do keep in touch. Good bye for now. With love. Patrick.'

Beth could hardly contain her eagerness to tell her mother and Anne and ran downstairs. 'Look mother I have a letter from Patrick, he said to keep in touch and that everyone missed us in Devon and Oh, mother, do you think we can visit them one day soon,' she beamed.

'I don't think that will be possible at the moment dear but you will be able to ' save some of your wages when you start work and perhaps you and Anne might be able to go,' she said, trying not to dampen her spirits.

'I will try and save every penny,' Beth said, determined she would go and felt there was hope. Beth hoped to obtain work in an office, her mother had enlisted her at a local night school for a Pitman's shorthand typing course, which she enjoyed and felt it was going well. Secretaries with knowledge of shorthand received a Little extra pay than those who could only type.

Clutching her letter she returned to her room to read it once again. 'How are things going for you?' she read. If only he knew what it was Like in this house. How would she explain to him how miserable they were and the fact that she was not happy or settled? It was not just strange being away from the farm it was unbearable. 'Oh, we miss you all too,' Beth thought as tears misted her eyes. Beth missed hearing Patrick's beguiling Devonshire accent, the chemistry between them and she thought of their last day together. Beth remembered staring into his kind brown eyes and promised she would return as soon as she could. They had walked to the gate together his fingers linked in hers. 'We will keep in touch,' she cried aloud. That evening Beth shared her letter with Anne, who was happy that Beth had heard from Patrick and agreed that it would be good to get away and to see aunty Rose and uncle Walter again.

Some weeks later the girls had another surprise. Mother said grandma had asked to see them. They arrived at her house wondering what could be the matter. Grandma smiled and seemed very happy to see them. 'Come in girls I have something for you,' she announced with an air of excitement.

The girls looked at each other and wondered what her eagerness was all about. Grandma began to explain. 'When you were born I took out a 'Pearl Insurance Policy' for you both and your brother to coincide with you leaving school and as you are in your last weeks of school, Beth and I heard you desperately wanted to visit that farm in Devon, I want you both to have this money now. You deserve it as you have both done so much to help your mother as well as having to suffer that father of yours.'

'Grandma, how wonderful, I can hardly believe it. Thank you so much,' cried Beth, giving her grandma a hug. Anne also thanked her very much but looked a little worried.

'I know what you are thinking my dear but don't you worry about your father, if he says anything to stop you going, he will have me to deal with. It is my money and I'll do what I like with it, he knows he cannot bully me. Your mother has told me everything and I think it will do you both good to get away for a while.' exclaimed grandma.

On returning home Beth was still in a daze. 'I cannot believe it, could this really be happening,' she said, taking her sister by the arm. 'I believe it is, I can hardly take it in myself, replied Anne. Beth was excited as she told their mother the news, who was so happy for them and said she would tell father when he came home. 'There are things to do and arrangements to be made but all in good time. You have to first finish school Beth,' she said trying to calm her excitement.

'I have only five more weeks before that day comes and I can hardly wait,' Beth declared, trying to contain her feeling of joy, as she rushed upstairs to write to Patrick.

That evening after their father had his tea and seemed quite even tempered and all the family were present mother took the opportunity to tell him of their grandmother's offer to the girls. Father drew in a deep breath and then turned sharply to her and said it was a waste of good money and that Beth should be looking for work, not filling her head with such notions and was needed in the house. Mother said that she could manage and Beth had time to find work before leaving. It was their grandma's money, she continued and that is what she wanted. Gazing sternly at his wife and raising his voice replied. 'Silly bitch, your mother is always interfering, well don't expect me to have anything to do with it,' with that he pushed his plate across the table, got up and stormed out the room.

The weeks that followed seem to drag at school for Beth and she noticed more than ever that the boys in her class got special attention so was glad to be leaving. The teachers said that they would be the bread winners of the future and so needed all the education and help they could get, whereas the girls had to prepare themselves for marriage and bearing children. The girls were given rubber dolls to wash and clothe and emphasis was given to cooking and how to run a household. This irritated Beth who felt everyone should have equal opportunities but she was happy knowing she could become a shorthand typist and if her dreams come true, she had already been schooled in farming and that was really all that mattered to her. Beth could still not see herself living in a town forever.

It was late July when Beth celebrated the end of her last term at school and mother had found in the local paper a vacancy for work in the office of Wag horn Brothers, a jewellers shop in Croydon. 'I'm sure that will be a good start for you Beth,' said mother who was happy she had found a position for her. She accompanied Beth for an interview the following day. The manager said Beth could have the post and was very obliging when mother explained that Beth had booked her holiday and could not start work right away. He said that was alright, as he was going away himself with his family. His two children were on their school holiday but he would be back in time for when Beth returned.

Mother wrote to aunt Rose and arrangements were made for the girls to visit the farm at the end of August for three weeks. Grandma had given them twenty pounds each so that they had enough money for their train fares and also they were able to buy themselves a new winter coat each and extra clothes for their holiday. Ronald wanted to go too but mother explained to him that his chance to go would come later when he was older.

The day arrived when the sisters found themselves waving goodbye to their mother and Ronald at the station. Father was at work and so any difficult situation was avoided. The journey gave the girls a chance to talk and Anne confided in Beth a secret she had been keeping to herself. 'I have met someone and have been going out with him for some time. His name is Donald,' she explained. 'Oh, that's wonderful. Where did you meet him? Tell me all about it. What is he like?' asked Beth full of excitement.

Anne described Donald as being very handsome with dark wavy hair and blue eyes and he was two years her senior. He was working as a mechanic and had a motorbike. He had taken her to the seaside but did not want father to know about him, that is why she had kept Donald a secret. 'Not even mother must know, as father doesn't like her to keep things from him, he would take it out on her if he found out,' explained Anne. She went on to say that living on a farm was not for her; she had come to enjoy life in the town. She had been dancing and to the cinema. Beth was dumbstruck and promised not to say anything to anyone. Anne looked at her sister and thought to herself, how happy they were to have each other to confide in.

'You will soon be working Beth and will be free to do all the things 1 have done, 'Anne said smiling at her, as if to read her thoughts. Beth looked out of the window and a patchwork of fields that stretched out in front of her, she felt at ease and happy to see the open countryside again. It was a long journey but the time soon passed talking to her sister about their life at home and the future.'

'Look Anne, we are almost there,' Beth tried to contain her excitement. 'Yes and we must gather our things, I believe we are near our station,' said Anne being practical.

The train started to slow down as the steam hissed and misted the windows. When the mist had gone by, they could see some figures standing on the platform, it was Patrick and his father Derek. Eagerly the girls jumped out of the train and they all greeted each other with excitement. 'Mr and Mrs Bale said they were sorry they could not be here to meet you but you know how it is on the farm,' said Derek with a smile.

'That's alright, we understand,' Beth said with eyes only for Patrick.

Taking their bags Derek led them to his car. Patrick took Beth's hand. 'How well you look, thank you for your letters,' he said. Beth didn't know what to say to him and just smiled, she had waited so long for this moment and here she was numb with happiness. As they got in the car they all started to speak at once.

'I can see we have a lot of catching up to do. How is your mother?' asked Derek, bringing Beth back from her thoughts.

Beth found herself saying. 'She is kept very busy but is well, thank you and how is Mrs Clayton?'

'My wife is fine and is looking forward to seeing you both,' said Derek cheerfully. Patrick felt slightly awkward remembering the girls last visit to their farm. Anne seemed quiet, happy with her thoughts and was gazing out the window, looking forward to seeing everyone again. As they travelled up the winding lane to Lydacott Farm, Beth could see far in the distance uncle ploughing and then they reached the five-bar gate to the path that led to the courtyard. It reminded her of the very first time they arrived as evacuees when the geese and ducks flew everywhere. Soon they found themselves standing on the cobbled stones outside the farm kitchen door. The wild cats were still there among some chickens running around the yard. The sheep dogs were barking and greeted them, wagging their tails as if they remembered who they were. On hearing the noise aunt Rose appeared from the kitchen garden with a basket of vegetables. Putting the basket down she hugged them both. 'Come on in me dears. You must be tired after your long journey,' she said in her Devonshire accent that was a joy to hear once more.

The girls were too excited to feel tired. As they took their bags to their room Derek and Patrick left saying they would be back later, as they had some work to do. 'You know how it on a farm Beth, it's not like living in the town you know,' said Derek giving the girls a wink. They both felt at home straight away and were so glad to see the fire glowing in the open fireplace, giving out such warmth, that it gave them a feeling of contentment that they had not felt since they left. Aunty was laying the table for tea when they saw uncle Walter striding across the yard with his faithful dogs one step behind him. 'Hello there, how you be,' he beamed, with his welcoming broad accent. The girls rushed to embrace him as they had missed him so much. 'Welcome back, me dears, it has not been the same without you.'

The girls had just finished eating when Andrew and Patrick arrived. 'Hello Andrew, nice to see you again,' said Beth as she and Anne each embraced him.

'So glad you could come, we must make the most of your time with us,' said Andrew delighted with their welcome. 'Mother said would you like to come over tomorrow, she can't wait to see you either,' he continued.

'Well, let the girls find their feet first,' said aunty with a smile.

'It is alright aunty, we are here for such a short time and want to see and do everything,' Beth said eagerly.

'I will see they are alright Mrs Bale, we will not get them milking the cows just yet,' said Patrick, winking his eye at aunty. They all laughed, everyone was in such good spirits, Beth thought.

'What a difference from living at our house,' said Anne echoing her thoughts. It seemed to her that they rarely laughed at home. They were always dreading father coming in. Beth sighed. 'Oh dear, this is no time to be thinking of unpleasant things. I'm going to enjoy every moment of my stay here, for I do not know when I shall be able to come back again,' Beth murmured to herself.

It was a chilly night so the girls stayed in by the fire while uncle sat in his favourite chair with Sheep by his side while aunty did some knitting. They wanted to know all their news and then uncle told them about some of the things that had happened since they left. As he spoke Beth watched the comforting shadows on the wall made by the flames in the fireplace. She thought of her mother and brother and wondered why everything had to change. 'If only they could be here with us,' she thought. Then she remembered her grandma and how she made that wonderful moment possible. That night when the girls settled down to sleep it was if they had never been away. In the morning, the cock crowed and the yard was full of noise. Beth looked out of the window and saw the cows being taken out from milking. Some were drinking out of the trough. Uncle was calling to his dogs whilst aunty was trying to get by them with some eggs for breakfast.

'What a din but such a welcome sound,' said Anne getting out of bed,

'We should go down, I think we have over-slept, 'Beth remarked as Anne joined her at the window.

'What a wonderful sight, everything is just the same. It is if we have never been away,' said Anne thinking she could not wait to see the farm again.

Auntie's warm smile greeted them as they entered the kitchen. 'Ah, there you be, did you sleep well?

'Oh, yes thank you,' they replied together.

'Well sit you down, I'm sure you can manage a hearty breakfast this morning,' said aunty placing a huge plate of food in front of them. As she left them the girls looked at each other.

'I wish mother and Ronald could be here,' said Anne looking at her plate.

'I was thinking the same thing last night, I shall feel guilty eating all this when I know they hardly have enough,' replied Beth.

'Mother would want us to enjoy our stay so we must, Beth,' said Anne trying to reassure her sister.

'Come on now eat up. The lads will no doubt be passing this way soon and you must make the most of your time while you are with us,' said aunty, as if she knew what they were thinking.

Chapter 17
The Girl Friend

Thoughts of home were soon forgotten when the girls heard a dog barking and Patrick's voice command. 'Stay boy, stay,' as he and Andrew entered the room. 'Good morning, have you come to take the girls out to have a look around?' beamed aunty, knowing that they all could not wait to catch up on old times and see the farm again. Before the boys could reply Anne said they were ready.

'Off you go then, enjoy your day. I'll see you later,' said aunty going off into the kitchen.

'Would you Like to see our new foal,' asked Andrew. 'Mother is looking forward to seeing you.'

'Oh, yes, we did promise and 1 would love to see them both,' Beth replied.

It was a familiar scene when they crossed the yard to the lane leading to Mrs Clayton's cottage. Beth thought 'am I really here, is this really happening.' She looked over to Patrick who must have read her thoughts as his gaze met hers with a smile.

'Here we are, look there's mother,' said Andrew. Beth waved enthusiastically. Mrs Clayton stood by her cottage door with her arms wide to greet them.

'Can this be Anne and Beth, well, how you have grown and into such lovely young ladies,' she hugged them both Like long lost daughters.

'Mother, don't you embarrass them,' cried Patrick, seeing their faces redden.

'Well it's true, they are young ladies, I can't see them mucking out like they used to,' she said with her voice full of laughter.

'I won't mind, I have missed being on the farm,' Beth replied but Anne did not say anything, as it was something she would not like to have attempted again.

'Come now and see our baby foal, while mother puts the kettle on, I know you would like to see it,' said Patrick quickly changing the subject seeing Anne's awkwardness and knowing his mother could be right about her.

'Oh, he's lovely,' cried the girls. 'What have you called him?' Beth asked.

'Lucky, replied Andrew.

'I like that, it is a great name for him, he is such a beauty,' exclaimed Anne stroking his coat.

Turning to the girls Andrew said. 'We can all go out riding after lunch, if you like, I'm sure Patrick can arrange for us to have some time off. We are not too busy at the moment,' he explained looking at Patrick.

'I'm sure we can fit in an hour after dinner,' replied Patrick. There was no hesitation from the sisters who said how much they looked forward to it. They had learnt to ride before leaving the farm and hoped they had not forgotten.

'Tea's ready and I have some scones if you would like one,' came Mrs Clayton's voice from the kitchen. Scones and Devonshire cream, how Beth longed to taste them again. They sat down in her homely familiar room: it was as they had remembered it. Beth found it comforting to know nothing had changed but Anne did not share her enthusiasm. Mrs Clayton's hair bounced about her face, as she told the girls what had been happening on the farm and how hard it was after they had all left, their mother being such a great help to Mrs Bale. 'When the land girls left Mr Bale felt it very hard at first, missing their help especially at harvest time,' she continued.

The girls explained how difficult it was for them to adjust to their new life and how much they missed living at the farm. They made no mention of their father but said their mother missed everyone too. After thanking Mrs Clayton for her marvellous scones and promising they would visit again, they left saying goodbye to them all knowing the lads had work to do.

'See you later at the stables,' called Andrew, as the girls walked down the path to venture once again into familiar surroundings.

Beth was so excited she didn't know where to go first, 'Shall we walk to that little cottage, where that boy Richard lives, it's such a pretty walk,' suggested Anne.

'Yes, lets. I wonder if he and his mother will recognise us,' laughed Beth, as she thought of their first meeting. 'Do you think he has found a steady girlfriend yet? Anne remarked with a smile. 'We shall see,' said her sister with a cheeky grin. It was a bright sunny autumn day making it a pleasant scenic walk. They could not help thinking how different it was from the war torn streets of Croydon. The thought of their house made Beth shudder. At that moment the cottage came into view.

'Look there it is, Littlewood Farm and just as it was the last time we were here,' exclaimed Anne. Suddenly Richard appeared at the door, as big and round as ever.

'Hello there, so you have come back to us, eh!' He beamed.

'Not to you exactly,' Beth thought to herself. 'It is such a lovely day for a walk and we thought it would be nice to visit you and your mother, is she keeping well?' Beth asked, feeling awkward.

'Well enough,' he replied. Mrs Higgins hearing voices called out. 'Don't keep people on the door step, Richard.'

He moved aside and they squeezed by him almost tripping over him as they entered. 'Why it's Anne and Beth, my how you have changed, quite the young ladies now,' she said gesturing to her son to clear chairs for them to sit on. 'You've got used to living in a town now I expect. Richard hasn't found a young lady yet, not like that young Patrick, I hear he has one in his sights,' she continued. Beth sat down almost in a faint, after hearing Mrs Higgins' news.

'Are you keeping well?'Anne asked not knowing what to say after seeing Beth in distress.

'Well enough my dear, I get the odd twinge but I don't complain, do I Richard?' she said looking at her son.

'No, mother,' he blustered, biting into a cake he had just snatched off the table.

'I see you still like to cook, I'm afraid I'm not very good at it,' explained Anne feeling quite on her own, as Beth was sitting in her chair looking numb. 'Well that wouldn't do for my Richard' she thought, still thinking of a future wife for her son. 'Would you like some tea?' asked Mrs Higgins as she went to put the kettle on.

'Oh, no thank you, we only stopped to say hello on our walk, we will visit again if we may 'Anne said politely and taking her sister by the arm, said goodbye. As they left, they heard Mrs Higgins voice in the distance.

'They're a strange pair, didn't even stop for a cup of tea or chat, I will never understand town folk.'

Anne turned towards her sister. 'Are you alright Beth, I know you are upset over what was said about Patrick. That was a bomb shell wasn't it?'

'Oh, Anne do you think he has a girlfriend, I mean a serious girlfriend?' cried Beth.

'I don't think so, we have not been here long enough to know but I'm sure he would have mentioned something in his letters to you,' said Anne trying to reassure her.

They arrived back just in time for dinner. 'Did you have a nice morning girls,' asked Mrs Bale.

'Yes thank you, we walked to Mrs Higgins' farm, the views are lovely, so different from what we are used to. 'Anne answered while Beth went upstairs.

'Is anything wrong?' asked aunty, concerned to see Beth walking upstairs looking quite forlorn.

'We have just heard that Patrick has a girlfriend,' said Anne as she looked at Mrs Bale for her reaction.

'I have not heard so and I think I would know as you can't keep a secret on a farm,' she smiled reassuringly. 'Tell Beth to come and have some dinner. Mrs Higgins has got it all wrong I'm sure and it wouldn't be the first time I assure you,' replied aunty.'

Anne went up to find Beth sitting looking out of the window her eyes were red from crying. 'Beth, don't get upset' Aunty said she has not heard anything about Patrick having a girlfriend and you can't keep a secret on a farm you know,' said Anne repeating auntie's words.

'But...but someone must have told her,' remarked Beth still unconvinced, her head full of questions.

'I think she must have misheard, I'm sure Patrick would have told you before we came, so cheer up Beth, let's go down. Aunty is waiting to give us some dinner,' Anne remarked putting her arm around her sister to comfort her. Both girls went down and for the time being, aunty seeing how upset Beth was, said no more about it.

'Are you going to meet the lads this afternoon?' she inquired putting dinner on the table for them.

'Yes aunty, we are going out riding and said we would meet them at the stables,' replied Anne.

'I'm sure you will enjoy that, mind you don't fall off, we don't want to send you home with any broken bones,' she said with a smile, as she cleared away the table.

Andrew and Patrick were waiting for them, 'I have saddled up Starlight for you Beth, we have not had him long. He will give you an easy ride and he has a nice temperament,' Patrick said reassuringly as he helped Beth up on the saddle.

'Oh, he's adorable, look at the star on his forehead Anne,' exclaimed Beth. 'He's a beauty,' agreed Anne looking at Andrew who led Dazzler to her. 'He is looking well,' said Anne stroking him, thinking how much she had missed him.

'Let me help you up,' said Andrew. He then untied the horses that were tethered at a post and turning to the girls said 'Patrick and I are riding Gypsy and Bramble, although a fair bit older I'm sure you remember them too.'

'Yes, of course,' came Anne's reply. When they were all mounted, they rode down 'Lovers Lane' to where the fields stretched out before them. They stopped and just gazed at the scenery.

'It is wonderful to be back,' Beth exclaimed and went on to explain to the lads about Wandle Park, which seemed a world away from them now Patrick looked at her thinking how she had blossomed into a lovely young lady and wondered how she could adapt to the hard Life of farming. As they cantered on, they were all enjoying the ride and being together again.

Mrs Clayton's Cottage

Chapter 18
Mixed Emotions

It did not seem long before they were trotting across the courtyard back to the stables. The girls helped to unsaddle the horses and rub them down. 'Can we go out again when you have the time, 'Anne asked hopefully.

'It will be a pleasure, you are on holiday and the time will soon pass,' replied Andrew, with a nod from Patrick.

'I'm off to feed the animals, so if you will excuse me ladies,' Patrick said with a grin.

'Can I help you Patrick?' Beth wanted to know.

'You don't want to mess up your clothes and hands, thanks all the same,' he said, leaving Beth bewildered. He walked away deep in thought. Beth was surprised and disappointed, especially as she was looking forward to helping on the farm.

'What's the matter Beth,' Aunty asked her as she walked into the kitchen, looking downcast.

Beth explained what had happened. 'Oh, don't read anything into that Beth, he has the nod on in his head, that perhaps over the lapse of time and you now a young lady, that farming is not for you after all,' said aunty, trying to reassure her.

'But I have not changed, I want to help, I love being on the farm and all it entails. I have longed for this moment. What shall I do?' Beth looked at her anxiously for an answer.

'Best to have a word with him me dear,' said aunty thoughtfully.

'I have written to him and told him how I felt about farming,' Beth replied.

105

'Ah, but he had not seen you and there's the difference,' she said with a smile. Beth went to her room. Perhaps, she thought, he does not want me with him and there is some truth in what Mrs Higgins said about Patrick having a young lady in his life and she was so looking forward to this holiday. Beth was so upset she buried her head in her pillow and sobbed.

Later when Anne came in, aunty explained that Beth was upset over Patrick rejecting her offer of help. 'I will go up and see her,' said Anne hoping she could say something that might help the situation. Beth was still lying on her bed. 'Beth dear, you are too sensitive. I'm sure if you told Patrick how you really feel about working on the farm, he would be pleased to have your company,' she said trying to reassure her.

'Do you really think so, I have been looking forward to doing the things we used to do, when we lived here.' said Beth.

'I'm sure everything will be as they were so let us go out and enjoy the rest of the day' said Anne cheerfully, linking her arm in Beth's, as they strolled out the room.

No more was said as they went out to collect some eggs for aunty. Beth looked up to see Patrick in the distance driving the sheep with his dogs at his heels, striding toward the gate. A feeling of warmth came over her. Could it be love she felt for him? Her thoughts were suddenly broken as Anne called out, 'I think we have gathered enough eggs Beth. Let's go in.' Beth nodded and they walked toward the house when Anne, as if to read Beth's mind said. 'Are you getting serious over him,' looking in the direction of where Patrick was working.

'I love him,' Beth replied without hesitation.

'Oh, Beth, you cannot be sure, you are so young,' came Anne's reply although she had suspected what her sister's feelings were for some time.

'I can't stop thinking about him. Do you think he has someone else?' Beth said looking at her sister anxiously for reassurance once again.

'That was just silly gossip, you are upset. All this will be forgotten I'm sure, when you have had a chance to speak to him about what Mrs Higgins had told us.' Reassured at her sister's remark, they entered the house. That evening Beth went over to the stables. She always found it a comfort to be with the horses when she was troubled. From a distance Patrick saw her and followed her. He hesitated before he spoke as he could see she was upset and deep in thought. He marvelled at the change in her. Beth saw him coming and remained silent, feeling almost overwhelmed by him. 'I'm sorry Beth if I was abrupt with you earlier but things have changed, you have changed, I mean you don't look a farm girl any more, you...,' Patrick was swiftly interrupted.

'I thought you knew me, I told you in my letters how I felt about the farm. I have not changed, it is you that have changed and I know why,' she said angrily. The next moment she had turned away and had gone. Patrick was so surprised at her outburst as it was not like the Beth he knew. Her tone so shocked him that he just stood aghast. He was bewildered, rejected and wondered why she was so angry. He had only declined her offer of help and in a way he felt it was a compliment to her. He thought farming would now be too arduous and dirty, as he saw it, for the young lady she had now become and also the fact that the sisters were on a short holiday. He returned home to think about what to do next, as he certainly did not want to hurt her feelings or let anything come between them to upset their friendship.

Beth went straight to her room not speaking to anyone. She sat in her favourite place on the window seat, going over and over in her mind what had just taken place. She had calmed down and felt terrible about her behaviour towards Patrick. 'Oh, what have I done? What must he think of me, if only we had not gone to see Mrs Higgins everything would be alright, but what if she said was true.'

'Beth, what are you doing up here on your own,' asked Anne as she burst into the room. Beth explained to her sister what had happened.

'You really must get those thoughts out of your mind, especially as you have not spoken to Patrick about it yet. He must be terribly confused,' answered Anne, almost pleading with her.

'I will apologize to him tomorrow and hope he will understand,' Beth replied meaningfully. The girls once again went downstairs to spend some time with uncle and aunty before going to bed.

The following day Beth purposely went out to find Patrick. She wondered how she would approach him after being so abrupt, even unkind to him, especially after he had apologised to her. Beth dreaded the moment, what if he rejected her before she had the chance to explain! Patrick was attending the cattle with Derek and didn't notice her standing in the doorway of the shed.

There was almost a boyish youthfulness about him but he was no longer a boy but a young man, she thought to herself. He turned and seeing her there, hesitated for a moment before giving her a slight wave of acknowledgement. Beth waved back before Derek broke the silence.

'Good morning Beth, nice to see you, won't you come in,' There was an embarrassing silence. 'Not like you to be so quiet, anything up,' Derek asked.

Beth desperate to hide her feelings replied, 'I wondered if 1 could help you, it's been a long time sense 1 have done any milking,' she said.

Derek laughed and said he remembered her first effort. 'Are you still as sensitive Beth? 1 believe Andrew upset you at the time.'

Once again there was an awkward silence. '1 think all girls are sensitive,' said Patrick, as if to come to her rescue. Before any reply was given Beth took up a stool and Derek pointed to a cow waiting to be milked.

'You haven't forgotten how then,' said Derek, still laughing.

'No, I don't think so,' Beth replied trying to find the confidence to do it. In her heart she wanted to show Patrick that this is what she wanted to do. For Beth it was slow progress but the men didn't say anything.

'Let's stop for some tea,' said Derek, sensing things were tense between the young couple.

Patrick came over to the bench where his father was brewing the tea. His shoulders slumped, he half-heartedly said, 'How are you Beth, I didn't expect to see you here today.' Beth blushed.

'Oh and why is that? You know I like working on the farm,' Beth felt herself getting hostile toward him again so she quickly turned to Derek and changing the subject said. 'How are your new calves, I expect they are getting quite big now.

'They are nice and healthy, thank you' Derek replied and handing her a mug of tea asked her how she liked being on the farm again.
'I like it very much, you know 1 didn't want to leave and I still feel the same. 1 hate living in the town. Beth spoke knowing Patrick was listening and desperately hoping he would say something that would indicate he knew this to be the case. Looking at them both, Derek put his mug down and said he had to go out and would be back soon. There was an awkward silence, except for the sound of the cows munching hay. Patrick looked thoughtful, frowned and gazed at Beth. He saw her dark brown eyes, her lovely fair hair that he admired and reached out and touched her hand. She noted the warmth of his eyes and stepped towards him. 'I'm sorry, Patrick. 1 was so awful to you, 1 don't know why 1 acted the way 1 did, will you forgive me,' she said affectionately.

Patrick smiled, 'There is nothing to forgive, let us remain friends I'm sure whatever it is that has upset you, is all a misunderstanding. We cannot talk here but when I'm free we will discuss what the problem is,' he said.

Beth nodded in response as Derek reappeared with a large broom. 'I'll take that,' said Patrick and walked away sweeping the cattle shed floor.

Beth said goodbye to them both and returned to the house much happier than she was before but still puzzled. Let us remain friends, what did he mean?

Chickens feeding

Chapter 19
Andrew's Secret

Beth was still haunted by suspicion from what she had been told by Mrs Higgins. It disturbed her so much that nothing else occupied her mind. Her mood became noticeable and aunt Rose was saddened to think it was spoiling the short time she had with them. She decided to tell Patrick what the problem was as she knew from what Beth had told her, he must be bewildered at Beth's sudden behaviour towards him. Only he could reassure her, she thought.

Patrick was in the open barn, opposite the house. Aunty knew the girls had gone down to the orchard and took the opportunity to speak to him. Patrick was deep in thought as he attended the tractor. He was reflecting on his encounter with Beth when aunty approached him. 'May I have a word with you Patrick?' He looked up at her and nodded his head. 'It is about Beth, I do not like discussing her, when she is not here but she is so unhappy and I thought you would like to know what is troubling her.' Patrick nodded once again, too surprised to speak and having no idea what was going to be said. 'Mrs Higgins told Beth that you had someone in your sights, a special young lady,' said Aunt Rose feeling uncomfortable.

Before she could continue, Patrick interrupted her. 'Oh, no, there is no truth in it. So that is why Beth was so upset with me,' he said in surprise.

'I'm afraid it is,' aunty said with a depth of feeling. 'We will keep this conversation to ourselves, I will leave the situation in your hands. I know you will be sensitive to her feelings, she is still very young and vulnerable.' Patrick told her not to worry and thanked her. As aunty returned to the house she thought 'Poor lad, he hadn't the slightest idea what was troubling her.'

On reflection, Patrick thought of their meetings, Beth's youthfulness and her irritation when she thought he had serious designs on someone and then he thought of her letters to him. Was Beth getting serious about him? His expression was intense as he tried to consider what to do and with a deep sigh, he took the tractor out into the field, for now he had work to do.

A week of their holiday had already passed and although Beth was happy to be back with the Bales and in the surroundings she loved, she felt depressed thinking of Patrick and the distance that had grown between them. She wondered what to say to him, when she next saw him. Beth did not want to make it obvious the way she really felt toward him. It was mid-morning and Anne, sensing Beth's feelings and wanting to take her mind off things, asked her to come with her to the garden as aunty wanted some vegetables brought in for dinner. 'Our baskets are still in the scullery, I still remember the shape of mine,' she said with a broad grin.

'I remember mine too, it is the round one,' said Beth, feeling a bit brighter. Do you remember aunty buying them for us at Barnstable market? Those were happy times,' she said wistfully.

After dinner Beth went outside to find Andrew watering his horse at the trough. He gave her a measured look as if he was hiding something from her and then he laughed. 'You look quite the country girl in those dungarees' he said looking at her and making her smile. 'Would you like to come for a ride?' Andrew asked patting his horse. 'Gypsy here won't mind, you can ride him to the stable and I'll get out Starlight, he could do with some exercise,' he said, thinking she looked unhappy. Beth said she would like that and Andrew helped her up onto Gypsy, she looked down and met his gaze. She was glad to have him as a dear friend.

Soon they were both riding across the fields, Beth felt the wind in her hair and was happy as they galloped along together finally stopping under an oak tree to rest the horses. In the distance they could see the ploughed land with its neat furrows and could hear the sound of a distant tractor. 'That will be Patrick,' said Andrew. 'He hardly ever has time off now that Mr Bale is getting older and needs more help, he says there is more than enough to do. I do my share of course but there is no harm in taking a break now and then,' declared Andrew studying Beth's face and watching for her reaction.

In almost a whisper she replied, 'He seems to be avoiding me.'

Beth had never seen Andrew's expression so intense before and as he replied his voice agitated and knowing her feelings toward his brother said, 'Patrick is busy learning all there is to know about farming and can't think about any serious relationship with anyone at the moment. Like us, he is too young and not ready for any other commitment but his work.' Beth made no reply to his comment as it took her by surprise. He must know something she thought. Deep in thought they both continued their ride and were soon galloping back to the farm. Beth thanked Andrew and said how much she had enjoyed riding with him.
   Andrew replied that it was always a pleasure to be in her company. She did not realize Andrew's desire was to hold her in his arms, to tell her how he had always felt about her. He was jealous of his brother and it hurt him to see her so unhappy. Beth looked at him and thought how pleasant he had been and tactful not to ask her outright what was upsetting her concerning herself and his brother. Andrew helped her down from the horse and for a moment hesitated as he slowly let go of her waist. Beth felt a strange closeness she thought Andrew was so unlike his brother in that Patrick had a more serious disposition. He did not have Andrew's sense of fun but Beth could not imagine feeling the way she did about anyone else as she did Patrick. Andrew paused for a moment, put his foot in his stirrup, mounted his horse and without saying another word took hold of Gypsy's rein and guided the horses away. Beth felt sure he wanted to tell her something.

   After their meal that evening the sisters went over to their old swing that was still attached to the rafters in the barn. It was a place where in the past they had spent many happy hours. They were talking together when the girls saw Patrick striding toward them. Anne looked toward the house and said, 'I will go in Beth, I'm sure he is coming to talk to you.'

   Tactfully she got up and gave Patrick a wave before returning to the house. Patrick waved and approaching Beth began by saying he had not seen her that day and wanted to talk to her. He had rehearsed in his mind over and over again what he would say but now that he was looking at her he found it difficult to know where to begin. 'Beth I know you are unhappy and it pains me to see you so, tell me if I have said or done anything to upset you?'

Beth was direct. 'If I asked you a question would you answer it truthfully,' she asked him, feeling uneasy but she had to know. Patrick would have been upset by this remark, if he didn't know what lay behind the question. 'I would never lie to you Beth you can ask me anything,' Patrick assured her.

Choosing her words carefully, Beth asked her question. 'I was told you had a serious girlfriend, is that true?'

'Well, I thought so but I'm not so sure now,' he remarked, trying to keep a straight face. He did not mean to be insensitive but could not help himself.

'How could you, after the letters that have been written between us. You said you had missed me and you were looking forward to us being together,' she declared, with her eyes full of tears, she felt her heart was breaking. Beth quickly turned to rush away, when Patrick took hold of her arm.

'It is you. You are that girlfriend,' he said and then released her.

Beth stood transfixed and confused, her mind fall of questions, how could she have got things so wrong. It was me that Mrs Higgins had heard about, if I had not been so jealous... then she heard herself saying, 'but I offered to help you, to be with you and '.. .Beth was suddenly interrupted.

'I did want you to help me Beth, it was that you looked so different, so pretty, so clean and lady like, I thought you had changed your mind about working on a farm, until I saw you milking that cow,' explained Patrick.

Then they both fell about laughing at the thought of Beth trying unsuccessfully to milk the cow. Patrick put his arm around her, then checked himself for fear of being rejected but Beth smiled at him reassuringly and he responded by holding her close and kissing her gently on the lips. They hadn't notice the night drawing in until they heard Mrs Bale calling them in for supper. Nothing was said to embarrass them but everyone knew that things were going to be alright from now on, by the look on the young couple's faces. Uncle stoked the fire and made himself comfortable in his old chair. 'Well young Patrick, these young ladies may be on holiday but I'm afraid we are not and have a lot to do tomorrow, there is the last of the harvest to get in.' said uncle, thinking it was time for Patrick to make a move home to his bed.

'I'll be up at five as usual so I'll be away now,' said Patrick, having the same thoughts. 'I'll say good night to you all, thank you for my supper,' he said looking at Beth who followed him out. 'No more tears now,' Patrick said, taking Beth's hand to reassure her. Before she could reply, he had kissed her on the cheek and left saying, 'goodnight Beth see you tomorrow.'

Chapter 20
Friends

Beth felt herself blush as she walked back into the room although nothing was said but from the silence and the smile on her auntie's face, she realized that they had been talking about her. Beth said goodnight and as if floating on air went upstairs to her bedroom and in its stillness felt the comfort of their renewed friendship. Anne soon joined her and they talked about the happenings of the day until late in the night. The next few days were busy on the farm but Beth enjoyed being in Patrick's company as she helped with the harvest.

The sound of the tractor was heard in a far off field. Beth had soon finished her breakfast and was getting ready to help once again. Anne said she would join her later as she wanted to stay and help aunty prepare a meal for the men who were helping to bring in the harvest. 'Oh, I should help too,' said Beth feeling guilty.

'That is alright, you can help another time,' called aunty, from the scullery.

'Thank you, see you later' said Beth and before another word was spoken, she had flown by the kitchen out into the court yard. She made her way to the field where she saw the men working. Patrick and Andrew gave her a wave as she walked over to them. Beth was soon helping them stack the corn and as she did so she remembered how she and her brother chased the mice and rabbits that were hiding in the stooks. It seemed a long time ago to her now. It was a childish game and she was now a young woman, old enough to help in the field. The morning soon passed and before they knew it, they were sitting under the shade of a tree eating some sandwiches that Anne and aunty had made them. Patrick and Andrew sat with the men, Beth longed to join them but felt she should stay with the ladies. Mrs Clayton, aunty and Anne were going to stay until the harvest was gathered in. Beth could not wait until the evening as she looked forward to spending some time with Patrick.

'Are you tired Beth, it's been a long day,' said Patrick as they walked arm in arm down the lane together.

'Yes, but I enjoyed it, especially because you were there,' she said shyly.

'Do you remember when you were here for the last harvest, there was a storm and we all dashed back to the house,' said Patrick.
'Oh, yes, I remember everything about our time here and we were all so happy,' Beth replied, thinking of her dear mother and brother at home. Patrick, seeing his question had made her feel sad, put his arm around her and drew her close to him. 'I'm glad you could come back. We will try and make your last week a happy one,' he whispered. At that moment Beth could see Andrew standing by the field gate, as if he was watching them. He gave a wave before disappearing into the orchard nearby. Patrick made no comment as they walked on. Along the lane Beth stopped and picked some dog-daisies, she thought how nice it was to see wild flowers. Patrick smiled to himself as he watched her, thinking she was still so young. Beth stopped and gazed up into his face and smiled, he wanted to kiss her but he turned away. 'What am 1 doing,' he said to himself, then he found himself making an excuse saying he must return to the farm as he had things to finish before the day was through.

'I'm sorry Beth but I still have a lot to do. You know how it is with work here, there are things that must be done before I turn in.' he said.

Despite her efforts she could not smile, it had been such a short walk and she felt she had so much to tell him. 'I understand, as uncle said we are on holiday but you have things that must be done,' replied Beth, hiding her disappointment. There was a moment of silence as they walked on their arms were not linked as before. Beth could see Patrick was deep in thought. What can be troubling him, she wondered as they reached the farm house. Patrick turned and kissed her on the cheek. 'Good night, Beth, see you tomorrow,' he said turning away and before saying another word, he was striding across the courtyard towards the barn. Beth stood confused, had she done something wrong?

That night, disillusioned, Beth lay in bed waiting for her sister. She glanced around her bedroom, wondering what had happened. Beth had not been prepared for Patrick's sudden dismissal of her. She loved him and could not imagine life without him. When Anne arrived Beth told her of her feelings. 'But Beth you are still very young, what can you know of love,' she queried. Beth sat up and stared at her sister, her mind a blank.

'Does Patrick know how you feel about him, has he said he loves you?' remarked Anne.

Beth was surprised at her sister's reaction. 'No, he has not actually said so but I feel he does. He kissed me on the lips,' she said trying to convince her sister.
'Oh, Beth, I don't want you to get hurt, men say and do things without thinking about them, well not as deeply as we do, on the spur of the moment. I'm sure he is very fond of you but he may not be seriously thinking of you in the way you think of him,' explained Anne.

Beth could not speak, she felt too confused and upset.

'Beth dear, I'm a little older and more experienced than you, 'Anne continued and 1 know we can easily misread the caring affection of a friend, especially men friends. Beth thought about what Andrew had said to her and wondered if he was trying to tell her something? She thought of the past few wonderful days spent working with Patrick. Surely he felt the same way as she did but Anne was right he had not said he loved her and he only kissed on the cheek tonight. Oh, what shall 1 do? The realization of life without him or living anywhere else but on the farm suddenly struck her. 1 wish mother was here, I'm sure she would reassure me that everything will be alright. Beth lay waiting for daylight to break, she had hardly slept at all that night.

The morning passed when Beth found herself aimlessly walking near the stables again. The feeling to be near to the things that were part of Patrick enveloped her, when suddenly she heard voices. Not wanting to be seen Beth stood riveted behind the stable wall. Beth recognised the voices of Andrew and Patrick arguing. 'You owe her an explanation,' said Andrew.

'I don't want to hurt her feelings,' replied Patrick.

'You are confusing the girl by being such a coward,' shouted Andrew getting angry, 'tell her you have come to realize she is too young to have a serious relationship with,' he continued.

'It is not only that she is so young, oh, I don't know what the future holds,' Patrick was trying to keep calm. 'I'm very fond of her and enjoy her company but marriage, no it is too early to think of Beth or anyone in that way,' he muttered.

'You must have given her that impression, what are you going to do about it?' bellowed Andrew.

Beth stood, shocked with mixed emotions, as she overheard them arguing about her. Anne was right Patrick did not love her. Beth realized how naive she had been and her next thought was she must get away before she was seen. As she moved, Andrew's horse that was tethered outside neighed, Beth ran as quickly as she could along the path to the courtyard. 'Whatever is the matter,' Mrs Bale exclaimed as Beth rushed past her into the house. She knew Beth was upset and what might be the cause, as she saw Andrew and Patrick appear in the distance.

The lads approached her and explained what they thought had happened. 'Oh, well, it is for the best. The girls will be going home the day after tomorrow and in time Beth will come to realize that she has a lot of growing up to do and maybe in the future, her dreams might come true,' explained Mrs Bale smiling at their worried faces. 'Come over this evening, we are having a get-together to send them on their way I will have a word with Beth. We don't want the girls to leave under a cloud, do we,' Mrs Bale said reassuringly.

'Thank you, I did not mean to hurt her feelings, I want us all to stay close friends.' Patrick replied sheepishly. On returning to the house Mrs Bale went upstairs and found Beth upset, sitting on her bed, as she entered the room Beth cried out, 'I feel awful, what must they think of me?'

'Now, now, they are both very fond of you and are thinking of your happiness.' Aunt Rose sat by Beth's side and as her mother was not there she tried to comfort her, to help and advise her about her feelings and hopes for the future. When Andrew and Patrick came over that evening all disagreements were forgotten, as they remembered only the happy moments of their holiday.

The following day Beth awoke with the realization that things would never be quite the same again. She needed time to think things through, to work things out.

'1 am glad we are returning home tomorrow,' Beth thought as she reluctantly went out on to the courtyard hoping not to bump into anyone. There was a sound of voices coming from the barn, Beth felt uneasy when she realized it was Patrick and Derek looking at some machinery. 'Good morning, Beth, this will be a sad day for you,' called Derek.

'Yes, 1 will be sad to leave,' Beth replied, as Patrick smiled at her sympathetically.

Beth hesitated for a moment unable to speak. Then with a wave she turned and quickly walked away. She went to the stables for the last time. The horses were such a comfort to her. Beth thought about how she enjoyed the long warm days spent riding out in the open, when she heard a horse neigh as if in agreement with her. Beth put Patrick to the back of her mind as she looked at the harness and equipment in perfect order around her. They hung on the wall with published horse brasses that seemed to sparkle. She thought what great pride the men had for them and how much she would miss being part of their world. Beth gave Dazzler a hug but could not bear to say goodbye as her eyes became full of tears.

Beth knew the harsh reality that was awaiting her in Croydon and that time would soon be upon her. She wished she could feel happier but was glad of a Little solitude in the stable as she thought about the future and began to feel more confident. Beth was determined that she would return and this gave her courage to face the rest of the day. On leaving the stable she returned to the house and was thankful that the men had left the barn. 'There you are Beth, Anne was looking for you, I believe she needs your help with some packing. 'Aunty called out from the kitchen.

'Thank you, I will go up right away,' replied Beth, feeling guilty that she had gone out before helping her sister to pack and finding it hard to believe that three weeks had already passed. It was a sad farewell as they stood outside the farmhouse. The girls thanked aunt Rose and uncle Walter for letting them come to stay. Aunty said not to let it be too long before they return again and uncle wished the same and laughing said, 'especially if Beth improved her milking skills.' Patrick and Andrew entered the courtyard saying that Derek was ready and waiting at the gate with his car. They picked up the cases as the girls waved goodbye and followed the lads to the farm gate. The friends embraced each other with promises to keep in touch and soon with heavy hearts they were on their way home once more.

Chapter 21
Future Hopes

Two years had passed since the day Anne and Beth returned home from Lydacott farm. Their mother was pregnant again after giving birth to a daughter just a year ago, she named her Rosemary. Grandma said, being pregnant was father's way of keeping her daughter in the house. 'Your father has become more possessive and heaven knows how many miscarriages your mother has had and how many more children she will have to bear, poor dear,' said Grandma to the girls when they visited her. Grandma was known for speaking her mind, especially where father was concerned, as she didn't have a good word to say about him. They barely spoke to each other as she considered him the lowest of the low, intolerable, the very thought of him angered her.

Beth was now working in the office of Wag horn Bros, the jewellers in Croydon. She enjoyed working there but helped in the shop whenever she could, as she enjoyed meeting people. Beth admired the beautiful jewellery but as she only earned £3-5-0 a week and most of that was given to help her mother she would never own one of the pieces of jewellery, partly as she had already started to save for the future. She had bought a money box and put it in a drawer in her bedroom. Life at home didn't get any easier especially as their mother was heavily pregnant. The sisters had more chores than ever to do and soon became efficient at cooking. Beth was now seventeen and although she went out with one or two boys she never thought of them in a serious way. Her heart was set on returning to the country. Anne was still courting Donald and one evening she told mother that they planned to marry.

'What will your father say, oh do break it to him gently,' was mother's sudden reaction.

'What can he say, 1 am almost nineteen. I can't wait to tell him or to get away from this house. 'Anne's response to her mother's fear of what her father would say irritated her. She expected her mother to say how happy she was for her. 'I'm not afraid of him.' She was about to continue when their father came in. Anne did not flinch from her father's stern gaze.

'Now, have you anything more to say?' He shouted having overheard what was said.

'Yes, father, I'm going to get married and you can't stop me.' She answered firmly.

The next moment Anne felt a slap across her face, she staggered and held on to the back of a chair. 'This is my house and whilst you are still in it, you will do as I say,' he demanded, his face flushed with temper.

Mother watched them staring at each other, then Anne recovering from the shock of being slapped bravely retaliated. 'That is the last time you will lay your hands on me, I'm leaving tonight and 1 pity mother who has no choice but to suffer you and your vile temper.'

Father's expression never softened as he marched out of the room shouting, 'Don't expect me to come to your wedding or have anything to do with it and 1 don't want him in this house,' he bellowed as the door slammed behind him. Her baby sister began to cry and as mother comforted her they heard Ronald's voice. 'Are you going for good?' as it echoed from where he was hiding in the kitchen.

'Yes, Ronald I'm going for good,' replied Anne with strength of feeling.

He looked at her in disbelief. He would miss her. 'You will come back and see us, won't you,' he said, trying to accept the fact she was leaving.

With a gentle smile Anne turned away from him, she turned her head in an effort to fight back her tears. An awkward silence fell on the room. 'Of course I will come back and see you, when father isn't here,' she assured him and knowing she would miss her family.

'Where will you go, you can't leave tonight.' Mother said anxiously.

'I'm going to Donald's father's house he said I could stay there anytime I needed to. Donald's mother died when he was young and he lives with his father. He has a brother and sister who are already married. I'm sorry mother I can't stay in this house a minute longer with him. He has never liked me for some reason and as soon as we see each other there is tension between us,' explained Anne feeling sorry for her mother but at the same time knowing that her feelings for her father had worsened over the years. Her resentment against him grew because of the way he treated her mother and all the family. 'I'm just a thorn in his side, he will be glad to see me go,' continued Anne. She went over to her mother who was looking tired and distressed and put her arm around her. 'I shall miss you all but I shall come and see you when I can.' Anne was too upset to say any more and tearfully left the room.

Beth followed her to their bedroom. 'It is awful you going like this and at night too. I shall miss you, it has been such a comfort to have you around, someone to confide in, as only sisters can,' exclaimed Beth.

'I shall miss you Beth but we can still confide in each other. We are different in many ways, you and I, you love the country, the fresh air and all that the country offers. A farm does not appeal to me. I like the town with its shops and everything to hand. Farming is hard work but you never seemed to mind. I prefer a more comfortable life,' she said smiling giving her sister a hug.

Beth didn't know what the future held for her but she knew she would be needed at home more than ever now that Anne was leaving and a new sibling about to be born. Beth helped Anne pack a few overnight things. She would be back for her other belongings tomorrow.

That night Beth felt restless sleeping alone as she did not like the feeling of separation from her sister. She thought about Anne and how happy she would be married to Donald. Fie was opposite to father in every way. He was a quiet, handsome man with laughing blue eyes, with a loving and caring nature. He adored Anne from the moment they met. Mother was very fond of him. Beth suddenly thought of Patrick, she had not heard from him for over six months and then he only spoke about the farm. She wondered if he had forgotten her. The last she heard was that he was going on a farm management course in Barnstable. Aunty wrote to say that Andrew was now working full time on the farm and was such a help to uncle, who could not manage as well as he used to. Beth wished things could have stayed the way they were before the war ended, she was happy then.

Two months later a bed was put in the front room of the house and mother gave birth to their baby brother. She named him William after her father. The house still felt strange to Beth without Anne being there but she often came when she knew father was not in. Mother was always pleased to see her and to know she was happy. The girls would often meet in town keeping up to date with their news. Beth would tell her sister how she was coping at home, now that there were two young siblings to care for and if mother was well. There was no need to ask if father had changed.

'Poor mother, she looked worn out from work and child bearing, when I saw her last.' Anne said bitterly. Beth knew that they both could only see a bleak future for her and what made things worse there was nothing they could do about it. Beth thought there was one advantage of having to remain at home that made it worthwhile living with all the stress that her father put upon them. She was able to save a little money each week, which gave her some hope of returning one day to Devon. Sometimes when she lay awake at night and wondered what life would be like if she did not return. The pattern of life would remain the same as it had been since she returned from the farm. Her nights became full of imagining what life would be like to be married and then would come the unhappy reality that she had no idea what the future held for her.

The day came when Anne announced that she was getting married just before Christmas, 23rd December. The wedding would take place in a little chapel near to where she lived. Beth was thrilled when Anne asked her to be her bridesmaid. Mother was worried about the expense but Anne assured her that it was all taken care of. Donald's sister kindly offered to loan Anne her lovely white wedding gown and Beth would be dressed in a lemon gown made by grandma. Ronald was wearing his very first suit with a bow tie. Grandma had given him the money that she promised him when he left school. He had just finished his last term. 'He will need to look smart when he starts work,' she said.

The reception afterwards was to be held at Donald's house, where his family would provide the refreshments. Mother was happy and grateful that everything had been arranged but worried what father would say or do. Anne said it did not matter as he was not invited. She had asked a friend to give her away so there was no need for her mother to worry.

Father had nothing to say when mother broke the news to him about Anne's forthcoming marriage. He knew Anne had no intention of asking him after what he had said, when she left home. She had made it clear that she could make her own arrangements. Although he felt humiliated, he would not however confront her over it. He acted as if he didn't care and carried on as if it was not going to take place. He would make sure he was out all day on that day.

When the day came there was great excitement. A car came to take mother and the children to the wedding. Mother looked unusually happy and attractive in her new coat and hat that grandma had bought her. She was so proud of her daughters and wished Mr and Mrs Bale could be there to see them. Anne looked beautiful and happy in her wedding veil and gown and Beth too, looked lovely and full of admiration for her sister. 'Could this really be happening, Anne, her elder sister was getting married.' she thought. Anne was given away by her friend and she and Donald were married. Beth longed for her turn to come when she could be blissfully happy with the one she loved.

The following day was Sunday and father had gone to Petticoat Lane. Mother and Beth were still talking about the wedding when he came home. 'I don't want to hear another word said about that wedding. Do you hear me,' he shouted, cross that he had not taken part in it.

All went silent as mother went into the kitchen to fetch his dinner. Beth sat looking into the flames of the fire, when mother put his dinner in front of him. He started to eat it and then pushed the plate across the table shouting 'I don't want that rubbish, if you spent more time in the kitchen instead of dressing yourself up for weddings, I might get some decent grub around here.' He got up and knocked his chair over as he flew out the door.

He did not go to bed for the afternoon as usual but went straight out of the house.

'This trouble is because I went to Anne's wedding yesterday. He will get over it, don't worry,' mother said, anxiously looking at her children. Beth knew it was not the first time he had pushed his food away across the table, when it wasn't what he liked. Mother always gave him the best food and then we had something else and she often went without for our sake. Father didn't seem to care about anyone but himself and everyone suffered for it. He was never patient and always had the final word. Beth felt miserable and wondered how long she could bear it and went up to her room. She opened the drawer of her dressing table wondering how much she had managed to save but to her horror it was not there. 'Oh, no, who could have taken it,' she cried and rushed down stairs to tell her mother.

'Who would have done such a thing. Are you sure you have not moved it?' queried her mother in disbelief

'No, 1 have always kept it in my drawer,' answered Beth. 'There were some ten shilling and pound notes, oh what am 1 going to do, it was for my fare to Devon and ... 'Don't go on so, it is bound to turn up,' interrupted father, as he took his coat and left shouting 'and don't look at me, I have not touched your money. The money was never found but everyone knew who the culprit was. Beth didn't try to save again, she felt it was hopeless and could not see herself getting away.

Beth was too busy with going out to work and helping her mother to run the home to worry about her future. Another year had passed and it was just after Ronald's eighteenth birthday, when an event was to happen that changed his life. He worked as a mechanic at a local garage and had just arrived home. He struck father for the first time after being hit by him. Father had been out of work at the time and he was not in a good temper and on edge as he sat down to dinner Ronald was in a jocular mood and was trying to keep up the family spirits. He was not a child any longer and so spoke at the table. Father banged his clenched fist on the table and told him to be quiet as he had enough of his banter. Ronald sniggered and the next thing they knew was their father's fist flying into Ronald's face.

Ronald hurt and furious and being a big lad punched him back so hard that father fell backwards onto the floor. 'You won't hit me again. I should have done that a long time ago. You are nothing but a bully. What you have put mother through all these years and she has suffered it for our sake. I should have finished you off",' he shouted. Mother got up and held onto her son's arm, in case he struck his father again.

'Get out, get out of my sight and don't come back,' father boomed.

'I won't. I'm going to sign up for the RAF and whilst I'm gone if I hear you have touched mother again. I'll be back and there will not be any holding me back then.' Ronald replied, with blood streaming from his nose.

Ronald went to his room and packed a bag and told mother he was going to stay with a friend until he signed on. Father as usual after an upset went out slamming the door behind him. Beth tried to calm the children, Rosemary was nearly three years old and William was now one. Mother was distraught, not only over what took place but the fact her eldest son was leaving home. They had always been very close so much so that father was jealous of him. Beth put her arm around her and tried to reassure her that everything would be alright.

The following day there was a sense of relief when father did not mention what took place. Beth was dreading seeing him but it was if the incident didn't happen. Mother had told Beth not to mention Ronald's name as she didn't know what his reaction would be.

Ronald eventually joined the RAF and mother received many letters from him. 'I am happily settled,' he wrote. He explained he always wanted to be a jockey because of his love of horses but he was too tall as well as heavy boned to become one. His dream was to work with horses one day and in the future perhaps own one of his own.

Ronald's horses?

Chapter 22
The Surprise Visitor

Beth arrived at the jewellers, feeling very despondent and after trying to concentrate on her work to no avail all morning, she went from her office into the shop and as she did so a young man caught her attention. He spoke to Helen at the counter. 'May I have a word with Beth Mayfield,' he asked.

Beth recognized his voice and cried out, 'Andrew. Oh what a wonderful surprise. How did you find me?' Andrew swung round and they embraced.

'You look amazing Beth 1 asked your mother, it was easy to find your home from the station. You remember you explained in one of your letters,' he said smiling at her.

'Oh, Andrew it is so good to see you. Why didn't you tell me you were coming?' she said her voice hoarse with emotion.

'It was a quick decision. I will tell you everything when you are free,' he said looking at the clock on the shop wall.

'My dinner break is in about fifteen minutes if you will wait for me,' Beth explained holding his hand as if he was about to disappear.

'Of course I will, I'll sit over here if that is alright,' said Andrew making for a chair in the corner of the shop.

Beth returned to the office in a daze. Mr Frazer her boss, seeing how happy she seemed wanted to know who the young man was. Beth explained and to her surprise his face broke into a smile and he said. 'Be off" with you, I can manage here, we are not busy at the moment. I'll see you on Monday.'

'Thank you so much Mr Frazer, it is very kind of you. I will make up the lost time,' said Beth gathering up her things.

'I was young once myself you know and anyway you hardly take anytime off" so enjoy your weekend Beth,' he said as she left the room.

'Yes, thank you, Mr Frazer,' said Beth rushing out to Andrew, still finding it hard to believe he was there.

Beth could not wait to tell Andrew that her boss had given her the rest of the day off and she did not have to return until Monday. 'We shall have more time to catch up on all the news,' she said excitedly.

'Do you think we can have some dinner first,' said Andrew with a grin.

'Oh yes of course, I know of a nice place not far from here,' said Beth as she turned and said goodbye to Helen. Helen who was looking on in amazement and wondered if this handsome stranger was one of the lads Beth had told her about from Devon. As she watched them disappear down the road she looked forward to Monday to hear about him.

After ordering their meal they sat looking at each other not knowing where to begin when Beth asked if all was well at the farm. His eyes held her attention. Andrew always had a certain appeal about him. 'Yes, all is well but I have something to tell you but it can wait until we have eaten,' said Andrew not wanting to discuss what he had to say, until they were on their own away from the noisy restaurant.

After their meal Andrew asked if there was somewhere they could talk where it was not so busy. Beth said that as it was a warm sunny day they could walk to the town hall gardens. They walked along the busy high street Andrew thought to himself 'I now understand Beth's love for the country'

In the garden they found an empty wooden seat. Andrew took Beth's hand as they sat down, his voice was low, 'Beth I had to come and see you, to tell you about Patrick.'

'Oh, has something happened, is he alright, is that why you have come all this way, she cried anxiously.

'Patrick is fine, it is just the situation he finds himself in. I know how you feel about him Beth and I don't mean to upset you but there is no other way of saying it. Patrick is engaged to be married this spring,' explained Andrew as tactfully as he could, uncertain of what she would say. There was an awkward silence when Beth replied.

'I'm surprised he didn't mention anything in his letters, then why should he, after all he had made no promises to me.'
'I came to see you Beth, feeling the news would be better said than written in a letter,' said Andrew knowing he had taken the opportunity to see Beth.

'Did Patrick know you were coming to see me,' she asked.

'Yes, he always was a coward.' Andrew answered angrily, knowing his brother had never been honest with Beth.

Beth was not angry and that surprised her. 'He never said he loved me, you know, so please don't be angry with him,' she said, 'but he should have told me,' she whispered to herself.

'I'm so sorry Beth 1 know how you had built up your hopes and dreams for the future and I'm sorry 1 did not tell you 1 was coming. I had planned to visit London before returning and felt 1 must come and see you first,' explained Andrew, uncertain of what to say next. He wanted to say, 'I came because 1 love you,' but it was not the right time.

In the solitude of the garden they heard the bustle of the traffic all around them. Beth still could not believe that Andrew was there. Andrew put his arm around her. No word passed between them. They were both unaware how long they sat in the garden before Andrew said, 'It is getting chilly Beth shall I take you home.' Beth nodded and as they walked to her house, his arm around her waist, she knew she wanted to be with him, near Andrew at that moment.

When they arrived, they entered the kitchen. Mother looked pleased to see them. 'You found her then, Andrew,' she said.

'Yes, thank you and found a nice place to have dinner,' he replied.

'Oh that is good, whilst you have been gone I asked grandma if she could put you up for a while and she said you are welcome to stay with her as long as you wish. She is looking forward to meeting you as she has heard so much about you and Patrick over the years. Is that acceptable to you,' mother said with a smile.

'Yes, thank you,' said Andrew and looked at Beth. 'Would that be alright with you Beth or would you prefer me to leave,' he asked hoping she would not object.
'I would like you to stay, we have not had a chance to talk yet, have we,' she said feeling strangely happy.

'Grandma is expecting you both for tea so if you would like to go now, I think she will be waiting for you. I will get your father's tea ready. It won't be long before he comes home from work,' she said thinking it would be best if this young man was not there when he returned, as he did not like any interruptions when he had his meal.

Beth understood her mother's eagerness for them to leave, she knew her father well. Andrew could see him another time before he goes to London she thought. 'Shall we go Andrew, grandma does not live very far away, it will only take us ten minutes to get there,' she said linking her arm in his.

'Goodbye, Mrs Mayfield and thank you for arranging for me to stay with your parents,' said Andrew leaving the room with Beth at his side.

'That's alright, I will see you tomorrow,' she replied as she hurried into the kitchen, with Billy and Rosemary who were now getting up to mischief.

They soon arrived at grandma's house and as they opened the wooden gate Andrew admired the bright mosaic window box below the front window. 'Grandpa made that many years ago,' said Beth seeing his interest in the brightly tiled flower box. They entered the side door which was always left unlocked and led into the scullery where grandpa was shaving. He was using an old cracked mirror awkwardly perched on the windowsill. A leather strap hung on a nail to its side. As a child Beth was fascinated as her grandpa stropped his cut-throat razor continually up and down. Shaving soap covered his face. Then his face was contorted and twisted in all directions as he put the razor to his throat. Grandpa suddenly stopped and said, 'Hello, excuse me, do go in grandma is waiting for you.' A voice called out 'come in.' Beth opened the door that led to the dining room. Grandma was sitting in her favourite spot at the side of the table.

'Do come on in the pair of you, sit yourselves down and tell me what you have been up to. So this is Andrew,' she continued, as Beth gave her a hug.

'Yes, grandma, I was so surprised to see him, not knowing he was coming,' replied Beth. Andrew said hello and thanked her for offering to let him stay.
'How long do you hope to stay, my boy,' said grandpa as he came into the room, Andrew shook his hand and grandpa went over by the fire to his old rocking chair where Prince his black Labrador dog was waiting for him and rolled a cigarette.

'I have two weeks and would like to visit London for a while, 'Andrew replied looking at Beth for her reaction. He did not have to wait long for she gave a faint smile saying it was not very long, which gave him hope that she cared about him staying at all.

After they had tea and caught up on what had been happening on the farm, grandma asked Beth to show Andrew to her spare room upstairs as she found the stairs difficult, with her crippled leg that she had injured getting into the air-raid shelter. Once alone Andrew asked Beth if she would like to go out for dinner with him the next day and show him around the town. Beth agreed and said she would come and meet him at grandma's around mid-day. Beth spent the evening with her grandparents before Andrew saw her home as it was only a short distance to her house. He did not go in as Beth said she would arrange for him to meet her father before he left for London.

'Well, what is this all about, your mother told me you had that lad from Devon here to see you. What does he want?' Her father's booming voice came across the room as Beth walked in.

'I don't know exactly, he has not said except that he wants to visit London and took the opportunity to come and visit us whilst he was this way,' replied Beth, not wanting to tell him about Patrick. 'Can 1 bring him home one evening to see you,' she continued.

'1 suppose so. It all sounds fishy to me. 1 won't hear the end of it if 1 say no,' he said grudgingly giving her mother a disdainful look. Beth thought '1 don't want to bring him here but Andrew might take it personally if she did not invite him home. 'The following morning Beth told her mother that she was going out for dinner and would bring Andrew home that evening.

'Will you be bringing him home for tea,' asked mother attentively

'No mother, he is expected at grandmas I will bring him back later this evening, father would have had his meal by then,' replied Beth thinking it was the best thing to do, not wanting to cause her mother any more stress. Andrew was waiting for her when she arrived. He had a look of concern on his face and she knew as she had feared that her grandma had been telling him all her family history. 'Oh, what has grandma said and what must he think of us,' she murmured to herself knowing how her grandma felt about her father.

'Hello, Beth is everything alright,' said Andrew adding to her concern.

'Yes, thank you. Mother said would you like to come round this evening,' she said cheerfully, not to show her true feelings. Andrew replied he would as he had not seen Mr Mayfield since he came down to Devon for a short visit and then not really to talk to as he was mostly out with his father shooting.

'Do come and have tea with us before you go. Your grandpa is in his potting shed at the moment, at the top of the garden with Prince. When the sun is shining through the windows he often has a nap there,' said grandma.

Andrew found Croydon a crowded town with its many shops and trams noisily rambling by, not a bit like the peace of the countryside he was used to but he was with Beth and that is all that mattered to him. He did not realize what she was going through or had been through until her grandma had told him. He imagined she was devastated when he told her about Patrick; it must have shattered her dreams of being with him and of living on the farm, he thought. He wondered if she could feel the same way about him, as he had loved her from the very first moment he saw her across the courtyard as a boy when she first arrived at Lydacott.

Chapter 23
The Visit

Beth noticed Andrew's uneasiness while they waited for their meal. 'Beth is it possible for you to come and spend a few days in London with me. It is no fun visiting a place on your own and it would be nice to spend some time with you,' he said, stopping himself from saying 'because 1 love you.'

Beth hesitated for a moment, she was still feeling confused over her feelings for Andrew and found herself saying,'1 would like to but my mother needs me and I can't stop work at a moment's notice, thank you all the same.' As she had thought he had more than a liking for her. His expression showed plainly that she had disappointed him.

Andrew smiled and said, 'Oh, 1 see, is it that you don't trust me. Never mind 1 shall go alone and you never know I may meet someone.' He did not mean to say that but he was hurt by Beth refusing him. Beth did not reply and was thankful that their meal arrived to save her from any more embarrassment.

Beth was glad when they finally reached grandma's house and after tea she braced herself for their visit home. It was not long before they stood outside the house, Beth turned and seeing Andrew looking anxious at the prospect of meeting her father again said, 'we won't stay long.' Mother was sitting by the fire with William and Rosemary. Father was sitting in his chair by the table reading a newspaper. He did not get up as they entered but gave a nod. 'I've bought Andrew to see you before he goes to London,' said Beth trying to ease the tension in the room. 'Good evening Mr Mayfield,' said Andrew stretching out his hand. Father put down his paper and shook Andrew's hand but still remained in his chair.

'So you are off to London, you'll find it a bit different from where you come from,' he said. Beth saw her father's face soften and a smile appear. 'I expect you will see all the tourist spots but there is no place like 'Petticoat Lane' for interest,' he continued.

'I have not heard of Petticoat Lane. What kind of market is it?' replied Andrew sitting down opposite him.

'It's a big street market where you see and hear every nationality under the sun, I go every Sunday morning, I just enjoy being there,' father replied. Beth thought 'we don't enjoy some of the monstrosities you bring home.' Everyone was relieved that father was being civil and the evening passed without any unpleasantness. Beth made a pot of tea as her mother put the children to bed. The conversation continued until it was time for them to leave. Andrew thanked her parents for their hospitality and wishing them well, said goodbye. Outside he turned to Beth, 'I'm going to London on Monday Beth so tomorrow will be my last day here with you, I wondered if you would show me the park you wrote about, the one that reminded you of Devonshire,' he said hopeful.

Beth agreed that was a nice idea,'I will come down for you after dinner as I will be going to church in the morning. 'Andrew kissed her affectionately on the cheek and reluctantly left her standing by the gate. As he walked away Beth made no response, she felt numb and suddenly alone. She stood for a moment until he was out of sight before facing her father once again.

The atmosphere was heavy in the room as she entered. 'Don't tell me you're not planning something, any fool can see he is in love with you, I hope you are not planning to run off to London with him my girl,' he shouted.

Beth could see the troubled look deepen in her mother's face as she replied. 'He has not said he loved me and I have made no plans to go anywhere. I am not a child and I'm old enough to make my own decisions,' she said in retaliation.

'Your mother needs you she has not been well, stop thinking of yourself like your sister. She went off and got married without caring about us,' father said, raising his voice.

'As 1 said, 1 have made no plans, I intend to spend tomorrow afternoon with Andrew before he leaves for London on Monday,' Beth went over to her mother and kissed her goodnight and boldly walked passed her father and went upstairs to bed.

Beth lay in bed thinking about the events of that day and a strange anxiety came over her. 'Will 1 ever be able to get away? How could 1 leave mother to the mercy of that man.' She thought of Andrew. 'Any fool could see he loves you,' her father had said. Andrew loves me that must be why he came all this way. When she thought about it his interest in her should not have been a surprise. She remembered when they went riding together how he held her in his arms for a moment whilst helping her down from her horse and the closeness she felt toward him. Andrew had been such an understanding friend, taking her riding on many occasions to take her mind off Patrick. She thought about the time when she overheard their conversation in the stable and how angry Andrew was over his brother not being honest with her and all the time he must have loved her. Beth felt so disturbed she could not sleep and wondered how she could face Andrew in the morning.

The day was dry and bright as she arrived at grandma's. Andrew wasn't in the sitting room with her grandparents. 'Andrews upstairs packing Beth, I thought he was going to stay a bit longer, have you had words?' asked grandma.

'Not exactly, but there are things we need to think over and we both need space to do that so that is why I think he is going so soon,' said Beth trying to explain at the same time not knowing her own feelings.

'Oh, 1 see I thought it was something like that. He is a nice lad so we hope it all works out well for you Beth,' she said turning to grandpa who nodded his head in approval.

'I thought 1 heard your voice,' said Andrew smiling at Beth as he came in. 'I'm ready if you are. 1 can't wait to see this park that 1 have heard so much about,' he said.

'Come back for some tea won't you,' asked grandma. They thanked her and made their way outside.

There were not many people in the park as they walked over to the boating lake. 'Do you like to row Beth?' asked Andrew. Beth said she was not good at it but it would be fun to try so they climbed in the boat and laughed when it nearly capsized. Beth was right. She was not very good at rowing they were going around in circles. It was great fun and it seemed to break the ice and as they stepped ashore Beth suggested they look for the little hut she had told him about which she and her brother and found solace in when they returned from Devon.

As they neared the hut they could see the bowls club was closed and no-one was about. 'Let's see if we can get inside,' said Beth. Andrew tried the door and it opened. 'Oh I'm so glad, let's sit over here,' said Beth pointing to some old chairs in the corner. As they sat down Andrew said he could see why Beth found this to be a little haven away from all her troubles at home.

They sat in silence for a few minutes then Andrew took Beth's hands in his, and without hesitation said, 'Marry me, Beth, I love you, 1 have always loved you but you only had eyes for my brother and I nearly gave up hope until I could see he loved someone else.' He wondered what she would say to his sudden proposal. For a moment Beth was speechless as she looked at him and realized she had more than liked him for a long time. Beth could not remember when that feeling for him happened but she knew now that she loved him. Beth was young and confused over her feelings for Patrick and thought she loved him but never felt this way. Now Beth felt loved as she had never been loved before and with great tenderness and her heart pounding replied.

'I love you too Andrew, I didn't know it for sure, until you said you loved me,' she whispered. He took her in his arms and kissed her, '1 have been wanting to do that for such a long time,' he said not wanting that moment to end. For the first time Beth felt secure and happy.

'Will you come to London with me, we could get married by special licence if you wish, 'Andrew said eagerly.

Beth drew away from him, her expression intense, 'I'm sorry I can't leave my mother, she is unwell and I have my brother and sister to consider and.. .'Andrew stood up, frowned and felt angry.

'You will have to leave them one day. Oh, Beth, let me take you away from here. I know how much you would like to come back with me. I can't leave you now that I know your true feelings,' he said anxiously taking her in his arms once again and in a passionate embrace, they were oblivious to all that was around them.

Suddenly, Beth, in a panic broke away, 'I can't marry you, I'm sorry, it is not possible and I cannot say when I shall be free so please don't wait for me,' Beth cried as she hurriedly went out into the openness of the park, her eyes full of tears. Andrew ran after her but she did not wait so he followed her at a distance, knowing she wanted to be alone until they were out of the park. Beth knew Andrew could find his way back to her grandma's as the park was a short distance from her house. When Beth arrived home she went to her room and lay on her bed and sobbed. She felt her heart would break. The true love that she found was now torture. She bitterly regretted hurting Andrew which only served to intensify the pain. She did not know what the future held for her. For her there seemed to be no escape.

The following morning before returning to work Beth told her mother what had happened, she was sorry that Beth felt she could not leave her but said as soon as she was well again there was no need for her to stay as she could manage now that the children were older. Beth smiled and put her arm around her mother and tried to comfort her, 'please don't worry about me. There is plenty of time to think about getting married. The main thing is for you to get well and I shall stay here until you do,' said Beth trying to reassure her.

That evening Beth went to see her grandparents. She had to know what happened when Andrew returned from the park. As she went into the sitting room her grandma who was known not to mince her words said.

'What a silly girl you are, Andrew was deeply hurt but he understood the dilemma you are in. He has gone to London before returning home.'

Beth burst into tears as she tried to explain, but her grandma knew well the situation Beth was in. 'You are too soft for your own good, I know it is difficult for you my dear but you must think of yourself and Andrew and your future,' she said trying to help. She was very fond of her granddaughter and wanted to see her happily settled.

'1 can't leave mother and 1 told Andrew not to wait for me. That would not being fair to him,' replied Beth.

'Andrew knows your predicament, I made sure of that. Try not to worry, we will have to wait and see what happens. In time you will see things differently, am I not right William,' she said turning to her husband for agreement. Grandpa was a very quiet man but was very alert to what was going on.

'Andrew seems a decent chap Beth. You don't want to lose him, he is a man you can depend on, if I'm any judge,' he said thoughtfully.

'I know grandpa, but I couldn't have gone away with him, not now' Beth replied sadly.

'I know lass, but don't give up hope, life has its way of sorting itself out but I'm sure things will turn out alright in the end,' grandpa replied rolling up a cigarette and drawing nearer to the fire. Beth said goodbye to them both thanking them for having Andrew and being so understanding and all that they had done for her.

The little hut

Chapter 24
Troubled Times

Beth came to terms with the news that aunt Rose wrote that Patrick was married and had moved away to help run his father-in-law's farm near

Barnstable and Andrew, who now took his place working for uncle full time at Lydacott. Her mother's health seemed to have deteriorated while things continued at home as usual. That is how it seemed to Beth until she was told by her neighbour that father was seen out with another women and not for the first time. The shock was unbearable but she decided not to tell her mother. 'Oh, God, how could he, with mother ill after she had suffered so much and all father's doing.' Beth remonstrated to herself There was one person she feared must not hear the news and that was grandma. 'AH hell would be let loose and there was no telling what she would do,' she thought.

This year was going to be one that Beth would never forget. She avoided her father as she did not want to confront him with her mother there but what she was not prepared for was grandma finding out. On returning from work Beth walked into the sitting room, all was quiet. Mother was sitting in her usual chair by the fire and grandma was perched on another chair, angry, with her arms folded waiting. Beth knew who she was waiting for and he was due any moment. 'You knew didn't you Beth but you didn't want me to know,' she said looking very cross.

'I didn't want mother to know, she is so unwell,' Beth replied.

'I know that but he is not going to get away with it, the no good, good for nothing,' she said raising her voice. He's no good and never will be, 1 warned you, Clare didn't 1 but no, you went and married him. 1..., grandma was interrupted.

'I thought I could hear your tender voice down the road mother,' said father with a grin on his face, 'and to what do we owe this pleasure.'

'It is no pleasure I assure you and don't call me mother. I have just heard you have another women on the side, you animal. You ruin my daughter's life, make her pregnant I don't know how many times, ill treat her and now she is ill and you can't have your way with her, you go off" and find someone else. You disgust me,' said grandma, who was so angry. Beth thought she was going to throw something at him.

'It's none of your business, so if you don't mind I'm going to have my tea, hopefully in peace,' said father taking off his coat and sitting in his chair, ignoring her.

Grandma got up from her chair, giving him a disdainful look as she went over and kissed mother goodbye and as she went to go out of the room spoke to him again. 'Don't think you have heard the last of this, you will get your comeuppance one day, I'll see to that,' she shouted.

'I'm sure you will. Goodbye mother-in-law. Where's my tea,' he said, looking now at Beth.

Beth first went with her grandma to the front door and asked her to wait and she would walk home with her. Then she rushed back and found father's dinner ready for him on the stove. After putting it on the table she told her mother what she was doing and said she would be back directly. Grandma told her that mother had known that her father was seeing someone else for a long time and she was glad as it made her life more bearable. Beth was shocked to hear what her grandmother had said but when she thought about it, father had been less grumpy and much easier to live with for some time but she hated him for what he was doing.

Anne was also shocked to hear the news when Beth arranged to meet her in town but not surprised as she said father was capable of anything. She, in fact, thought he was seeing someone years ago! 'Where did you think he went when he walked out in a temper,' she queried. He did not have the money to drink beer and they have never seen him the worse for it. Anne asked her sister what she was going to do and Beth said she would carry on as usual for the time being; what else could she do.

A month later their mother had died. She was 49 years old. Beth and the family were devastated. On the day of her funeral Beth saw her father weep and heard him crying, 'what have I done, what have I done?' She felt little pity for him and thought, 'what haven't you done.' Grandma had no sympathy and said it should have been him!

With the passing of time Beth took over her mother's role. Rosemary was now 8 years old and William was 6. She was still able to go to work as the children were at school. Her next door neighbour had two children of her own and was able to look after Rosemary and William after school, until Beth returned from the office.

One evening Beth went with her siblings to see her grandparents. Her grandma was in a very cheerful mood. 'Oh I'm so glad to see you Beth, I wondered how I was going to get in touch with you, getting to your house is quite a feat with my old crippled leg,' she said with a smile.

'What is it grandma?' Beth asked wondering what all the excitement was about.

'Well it is to be a surprise. Can you come back on Saturday morning? It is good news for you all,' she told her grandchildren. Rosemary's smile Ht up her face and grandma always found her a pure delight with her trusting innocence and happy nature. She was always pleased to see William too, with his blond hair, blue eyes and cheeky grin.

'Life is a bit short on happy surprises,' said Beth philosophically, 'we shall be here.' Beth stayed with her grandma for a while. Rosemary and William played with grandma's old button box. Beth remembered the box being given to Anne and herself to play with when they were young. It had some old broken jewellery in it as well as attractive buttons that had fascinated them for hours.

Grandma's button box

Chapter 25
A New Encounter

On returning home Beth had another surprise waiting for her. In the sitting room sat in mothers chair was a lady waiting to meet them. Father got up as Beth and the children entered the room. 'I want you to meet Ivy, she has agreed to marry me,' he said bluntly, smiling at her and with no sensitivity shown toward his children he said pointing in their direction. 'This is Beth, Rosemary and William.

'Hello, I'm pleased to meet you as I have heard so much about you,' Ivy said awkwardly looking at Beth and then the children.

Beth was speechless, the children shyly stood beside her. 'Hello, I had no idea father was thinking of getting married again or so soon,' said Beth as politely as she could at the same time trying to hide the shock she felt that this was taking place.

'Well there is no reason not to, I have lost my wife and Ivy lost her husband years ago so there's no wrong in it. Ivy can help with the cooking and the children so that will give you some freedom. That's what you wanted wasn't it,' he said smugly.

'I see you have it all worked out then father. When do you intend to get married?' asked Beth wanting to know what else was planned.

'We thought next month, yes April, that will give us time to sort things out, won't it Ivy,' he said turning to her. Ivy looked very timid and quite small beside him. 'Yes, just the kind of person he could dominate, 'Beth thought to herself as she gazed at the slim but plain person who was still standing but now holding on to mother's chair for support. It was obviously not only an ordeal for Beth but for her also.

'I see, well excuse me I will get the children ready for bed,' said Beth leading them upstairs, without saying another word to either of them. Ivy did not stay for the evening; father had taken her home. Beth stayed in her room to avoid him but he did not return.

The next morning Beth went to work and thought about the situation all day and was glad that tomorrow was Saturday when she was seeing her grandparents.
She needed to talk to them. There was no way she could live in the same house as that woman, who was trying to take her mother's place. How could she leave her brother and sister with her especially after just losing their mother? What was she going to do? She longed to see Andrew again, to feel his loving arms around her, to help take away this nightmare that father had once again put on them but that was not possible as she had told him not to wait for her. Ivy did not come in with father that evening and he sat eating his tea without saying a word. Beth was in the kitchen. When he had finished he came out to her, 'Well what did you think of Ivy, you did not have much to say to her,' he said agitated at Beth's attitude.

Beth did not what a confrontation with him. 'Well she seems a nice person but I really don't know her,' Beth replied, holding her breath for his answer.

'Well you soon will as I have asked her to come and live with us in two weeks' time. That should be long enough time to organize things,' he said waiting for her reaction.

'It's your house you can do what you like, can't you,' she said, finding a new confidence. Beth had not been so outspoken to him before.

He could see Beth was not happy at the situation and raising his voice as he went out shouted, 'yes, it is my house and I will do what I want with or without your approval, my girl.' He put on his coat. 'I won't be back tonight,' he continued as the door slammed.

'Goodbye, I shall not miss you,' she said out loud when he had gone. Beth sat by the fire in her mother's chair for comfort, thinking how she missed her and what the future now held for them and how she was looking forward to tomorrow when she would see her grandparents again. Beth felt she needed their support more than ever as she did not know what to do. Leaving the comfort of her chair, Beth went into the front room where the children were playing. She sat at the piano and played a cheerful melody to help her state of mind, then, feeling calmer, she turned to the children and told them it was time for bed.. It was something she was used to doing and the thought of anyone else looking after them upset her.

The following morning Beth was feeling better and the children were excited to go to grandma's house. They were soon on their way and when they reached the house all seemed very quiet, 'Hello, grandma here we are and all quite excited wondering what the happy surprise could be,' said Beth joining in the excitement with the children.

'Well a part of it is in the front room so if you would like to go in first Beth, I will send your brother and sister in a moment,' said grandma looking at grandpa who gave her a wink.

Beth slowly went into the room not knowing what to expect. At first she saw nothing unusual when suddenly someone familiar came from behind the door, 'Oh, I can't believe it, Andrew, how, when ...,' she stuttered as she fell into his arms. For a moment neither of them spoke, they just held each other, not wanting to part.

Then Andrew said softly, 'sit down Beth, your grandma wrote to me and explained everything that has happened, I came straight away, I just had to see you, to be with you.

'But Andrew, I still can't come back with you, the situation is worse than before. Father is getting married, he brought his intended wife home and...' cried Beth. Before she could continue Andrew seeing how distressed she had become, interrupted her.

'I understand from what your grandma told me, what the real problem is. You feel you can't leave your brother and sister with them,' said Andrew taking her hand and sitting down beside her.

'I can't leave them with a stranger and at the mercy of my father. I'm sorry, I just can't,' she sobbed.

'Please, don't cry Beth. It is alright; your grandma explained that you might not want to leave them here and I agree with you. I have spoken to Mr and Mrs Bale and they have agreed that your brother and sister are welcome to come and stay with them and we are welcome too, until we have a place of our own. Mother also offered too, for us to stay with her at the cottage, so you see everything will be alright, that is... Oh Beth can I ask you again, will you marry me. Please say you will I cannot imagine life without you. I have never stopped loving you and have missed you so much,' he said taking out his handkerchief to wipe away her tears.

'I can't imagine life without you and nothing could make me happier,' said Beth nodding her head and smiling as she blinked away her tears. 'Can you ever forgive me for pushing you away, when 1 think about the short time we had together and how I treated you, I feel so ashamed, I love you so much, I have thought of no one else but you and the thought of living the rest of my. life without you has been unbearable,' she exclaimed.

'Then that is settled, you are ah coming back with me...' said Andrew but before he could continue Beth anxiously said, 'It all sounds wonderful Andrew, thank you for going to so much trouble but what if father will not agree to the children coming with us?' she added. Just at that moment the children came in and Beth gave them a hug. They were surprised to see Andrew and then Beth asked them if they would like to live on the farm in Devon, if father agrees. Rosemary and William knew all about Devon and the farm as their sisters were always talking about the wonderful time they had there.

'That was our lovely surprise wasn't it Beth. We would like to go wouldn't we William. You would like to go on a train and see the animals wouldn't you,' she said excitedly, looking at her brother. He shyly nodded his head.

'Let us go and see grandma, we have a lot to thank her for,' said Beth holding Andrew's hand thinking she was in a dream, 'I still can't believe you are here, I have missed you so much,' she whispered to Andrew as they entered the sitting-room, everyone was smiling. Grandpa said he would put the kettle on. It seemed to be the right thing to do at that moment.

'What are your plans now?' inquired grandma elated to see the young couple looking so happy.

'We have to ask father about the children coming to live on the farm,' answered Beth looking at Andrew once again.

'I will come and see him with you, and explain that we intend to get married and would like to take your brother and sister to Devon with us,' said Andrew.

'I don't think for one moment he will mind now that he has someone to look after him. He would have her to himself and have no responsibilities of caring for his children. It would make his way clear to do whatever he wanted. Your father will not believe his luck,' said grandma scornfully. 'I hope you are right but you know how awkward he can be. I expect he will be home now as it is Saturday. Shall we go and see him Andrew?' said Beth turning to him, feeling more confident knowing he would be there.

'Of course, if you feel up to it, this has been such an ordeal for you,' said Andrew with 'concern. Beth said it must be done and when grandma offered to keep Rosemary and William with her, until they returned in case of any unpleasantness, they were grateful and were soon on their way to Clarendon Road, not knowing what lay before them. The terrace houses looked more dilapidated than ever, as the war-torn gloom surrounded them when they approached the house. Beth could not help but think of the open countryside that awaited them and prayed that her father would see reason and let her siblings have a better life with Andrew and herself away from this dreadful place they knew as their home.

The Open Country of Devonshire

Chapter 26
A New Beginning

They stood outside the house when Andrew asked Beth if she was ready to face her father. She nodded, feeling apprehensive but felt safe with Andrew there to support her. Father and Ivy were sitting at the table smoking when they entered the sitting room. Father jumped up from his chair, 'Hello, what's this then, you didn't tell me he was coming,' said father surprised at seeing Andrew.

'I didn't know myself until I went to see grandma today,' replied Beth.

'I might have known she would have something to do with it, well, what's it all about? You must have come for some reason,' said father looking at Andrew.

'Yes we have,' said Andrew who could hardly hold his temper at her father's attitude. 'I have asked Beth to marry me and she has accepted,' he continued.

'Oh I see, so that's how it is. Well what about Rosemary and William, you have not thought about them have you. I need Beth here, I can't expect Ivy to take on the house and the kids, when we are not even married yet,' he shouted.

'We have thought about them and want to take them with us to live in Devon,' said Beth trying not to anger her father any more.

'What, you must be mad,' he bellowed.

'We will take full responsibility for them. They will love it on the farm and it will be much healthier for them,' she continued.

'What do you mean healthier for them, they are doing alright here,' said father raising his voice even more.

'Rosemary has a bad chest and allergies from the dampness of this house. The walls are wet in her bedroom and always have been. It is a wonder she does not have pneumonia,' retaliated Beth, getting as impatient as Andrew who stood earnestly by her side.

'I will have to think about all this,' he said looking at Ivy. Beth could see he was thinking of the advantages and began to feel sorry for Ivy who was feeling very uncomfortable, that was until she spoke.

'I'm living in a flat at the moment with my unmarried daughter and she is quite happy for me to come and live here. I was looking forward to helping you with the children,' said Ivy smiling at Beth.

'That is very kind of you but as we have just explained we are going to be married and live in Devon and want to take my brother and sister with us.' Before there was any response Beth turned to her father. 'We have said what we came to say and we will leave it with you to talk over. We shall go now and collect them from grandma's house and perhaps you will tell us your decision when we return,' said Beth determined to have the last word.

They left the house without a backward glance and when they were outside Andrew took Beth in his arms. 'Well done, you were wonderful,' he whispered. Beth gave a half smile and wondered what the outcome would be. Her grandparents were eager to know how the meeting went. When Beth explained what had taken place, grandma said. 'When they see how much better off" they will be it won't take them long to decide, you mark my words. Don't you worry Beth I know him of old, he always did think of himself first,' remarked grandma who had less feelings than ever for him.

After staying for tea, they all made their way back to the house. Father was sitting by himself. 'I have taken Ivy home, she felt what we had to say was our business,' he said with a stern face as he turned to Beth, 'I think it would be a good idea to put them to bed, they have had enough excitement for one day, I want to speak to your intended here,' he said looking at Andrew.

'His name is Andrew, father,' Beth said indignantly, as she took the children upstairs to bed.

'Well look here, ANDREW, he said sarcastically, do you fully realize what you will be taking on, I mean it is a big responsibility. If they go with you, I don't want you bringing them back here, expecting me to start looking after them. They have got to settle one place or the other. You can't mess about. You will be taking them on for life, having full responsibility for them. I won't be able to help out much with money, jobs as they are,' he continued.

'Beth and I have discussed all this and we are willing to take them with us for life, with no expense to you. They will have a good life in the country with excellent schools. We will keep you informed of their progress so you will have no need to worry about them.' Andrew spoke plainly and assuredly so much so that Mr Mayfield was taken aback and sat down.

'You have spoken to the children 1 presume,' he said. Andrew nodded. Father continued, 'Well that's settled then, when were you thinking of going back.'

'At the end of the week, that is in five days,' replied Andrew as Beth came in the room. 'Your father and I have talked things over and he has agreed that Rosemary and William can come to Devon with us,' said Andrew taking Beth's hand in his.

'You realize there will be no turning back once they leave here, it will be for good. The responsibility for their future will be on your shoulders,' said her father staring at Beth and then at Andrew.

'Yes, father and that is how we want it to be,' said Beth smiling at Andrew. Father left them saying he would not be back that night and said they must sort out all the arrangements.

'Oh Andrew can it be true, 1 thought he was going to be difficult and it was going to be harder than this to get his agreement,' said Beth putting her arms around him.

'As your grandmother said, he is only interested in the advantage to himself. He will come to realize one day what he has lost and then it will be too late,' said Andrew thinking how lucky he was to have the one he loved and knowing that she would be happy and content now that her siblings would have the chance to be happy too, made his happiness complete.

Beth's grandparents were thrilled and relieved to hear the news. It was just as grandma predicted. The time soon passed and the day came for the little family to say goodbye, with promises that they would return for a holiday with their grandparents in the near future.

Beth and Andrew were married in the Little church at the bottom of the hill. It was a day that they would never forget though tinged with the sadness that their mother was not there to see Beth happily married. Everyone agreed that Beth looked radiant and happy with Andrew at her side. Anne and Donald were there with their baby son Steven. Anne was her maid-of-honour, Rosemary her bridesmaid and William was their pageboy. Uncle Walter gave her away, as her father was indisposed. Patrick and his wife Mary came and in time they all became very close friends, letting bygones be bygones. Auntie looked so proud in a lovely new hat as she sat with Valerie and Derek. Mrs Higgins and Richard were also there and beside Richard sat a young lady as big and round as he was. Beth's day was made complete by the surprise arrival of Andrew's best man. Everyone knew he was coming except Beth, as Andrew wanted it to be a complete surprise. It was not until Beth was walking down the aisle that she saw her brother Ronald standing, smiling at her in his RAF officer's uniform. She was so overwhelmed that her eyes clouded with tears and it took all her strength to compose herself. Their wedding reception was held at the farm and to Beth's surprise Andrew had bought her a piano for her wedding present. It truly was the happiest day of her life.

Beth lived a full and happy life doing what she had always dreamed of. She was a farmer's wife, with a devoted husband and to complete her happiness, she saw her young brother and sister content and happy too, experiencing the joy of her own childhood. Much later, Beth's own family of three sons followed in their footsteps.

The years passed and with them came the sadness of losing first uncle Walter and then aunty Rose. As Mr and Mrs Bale had no children of their own the farm was left to Andrew and Beth. They knew how much Beth always loved living there as an evacuee and how she never ever wanted to leave. Beth vowed she would never leave the farm and she never did.

Milk churns

Mangold cutter

Tractor

Stacking hay

Living hedge

Collation of country life

Collie pup

Wild cats

Ferrier

Cow and calf

Pigs feeding at the trough Lambs suckling

Shire horses ploughing

Milking the cow Hay stack

Collation of country life

Water butt

Blackboard and Easel

Wireless

Hopscotch

Tin bath and bucket

Wicker baskets

Collation of country life

Elizabeth's novel in part, is based on her own experiences, providing a fascinating insight into wartime England as viewed through the eyes of a teenager. Emotions simmer below the surface as the story unfolds and takes a turn that is not easily predicted. One is also left to reflect on the' sharp contrast between life in the country and the day to day disruptions of air-raids nearer the cities. Through the text there is a sense of the reality and agony of the decisions faced by families during this vital part of our modern history.

Congratulations on your first literary exploit and perhaps I should add that I' am not the Patrick in the book.

Patrick Cox Smith

Made in the USA
Charleston, SC
20 March 2015